CHAMPAGNE COBBLERS
NORTHAMPTON TOWN
1986-87

ALSO BY MARK BEESLEY AND PUBLISHED BY DESERT ISLAND BOOKS LTD

ISBN
Northampton Town: A Season in the Sun 1965-66   978-1-905328-01-7

CHAMPAGNE COBBLERS

NORTHAMPTON TOWN 1986-87

Series editor: Clive Leatherdale

Mark Beesley

DESERT ISLAND BOOKS

First published in 2011
by
DESERT ISLAND BOOKS LIMITED
32 Lascelles Gardens, Ashingdon, Rochford, Essex SS4 3BP
United Kingdom
www.desertislandbooks.com

© 2011 Mark Beesley

The right of Mark Beesley to be identified as author of this work has been asserted under The Copyright Designs and Patents Act 1988

British Library Cataloguing-in-Publication Data
A catalogue record for this book is available from the British Library

ISBN 978-1-905328-94-9

All rights reserved. No part of this book may be reproduced or utilised in any form or by any means, electronic or mechanical, including photocopying, recording or by any information storage and retrieval system, without prior permission in writing from the Publisher

The author and publisher gratefully acknowledge Pete Norton for all photographs reproduced in this book

Printed in Great Britain

Contents

		PAGE
	Foreword by Alan Carr	6
	Author's Note	7
	Introduction	8
1.	A Steering Job for Carr	13
2.	The Watford Connection (I)	30
3.	Flights of Fancy	46
4.	Murder on the (Leyton) Orient Express	63
5.	Riding a Gresty Road Wave	93
6.	Newcastle – A Bridge Too Far	108
7.	Over the Hill and Far Away	124
8.	Swings and Roundabouts	137
9.	The Watford Connection (II)	149
	Guide to Seasonal Summary	153
	List of Subscribers	160

DEDICATION:
In piecing together this memorable campaign, it is fitting that I express my thanks to the huge input of historian Frank Grande and photographer Pete Norton, the unstinting support of my wife Caroline, and the memories of Cobblers past related by Tony Hiskey, my first subscriber.

FOREWORD BY ALAN CARR

Before I start, can I just say that I never, never, never thought that I would be writing the foreword for a book about football. Any other subject but football!

It's all a bit surreal, but then I suppose, looking back, the 1986-87 season was surreal in many ways. Believe it or not, Northampton Town FC felt like it was the centre of the universe – yes, I know Northampton and epicentre aren't two words you'd expect to find in the same sentence, but nevertheless the team was top of the then Division Four by a hefty margin. There were queues around the block to watch games and Cobblers fans before matches weren't just deliberating whether we'd win or not, but how much we'd win by.

Giddy times, I can tell you. I have fond memories of the County Ground. Yes, it was a bit ramshackle but it had its quirks, it was the only football ground that had three sides and a pitch that was essentially, let's face it, the car park for the cricket. Oh, and who could forget those signs which naively told the fans 'Please do not swear'. If you didn't know better, you'd think they'd shoved two thousand Tourettes Sufferers down the Hotel End.

I never got the chance to actually venture onto the pitch; one of my regrets was not being a mascot for the Cobblers. My brother Gary got to be one, though. He did it on the last home game when we knew we had gone up to Division Three. He ran on with the players up the tunnel. Sadly, he fell over. 'Gary Carr taking a bit of a tumble there,' boomed the voice over the tannoy, just in case you hadn't seen the little ginger kid fall flat on his face in the middle of the pitch. He's still mentally scarred from that to this day – poor thing.

But most excitedly, my dad, Graham Carr was at the helm – he was a god, he even had his own chants, 'Graham, Graham Carr, he's got no hair but we don't care, Graham Graham Carr,' with the obligatory 'ooh aah' at the end. And I would go to every home game and watch Trevor Morley, Richard Hill, Eddie McGoldrick strutting their stuff, and who could forget the mighty Peter Gleasure in goal. I would watch from the top of the stand behind the DJ, and if the game did begin to drag, sorry dad, but sometimes they did, I would whip out my trusted Agatha Christie and have a quick gander at that. You could always tell how good a season the 'Cobblers' had had by how far I had read through my Agatha Christie, and I am proud to say that during that glorious season of 1986-87, Hercule Poirot and Miss Marple didn't get much of a look in.

Up the Cobblers!

AUTHOR'S NOTE

The playing careers of Graham Carr and Clive Walker briefly overlapped at Northampton Town over the course of two seasons in the 1960s. It is curious to note that Walker claimed the No 3 jersey from Carr when making his debut after signing from Leicester in October 1966 in a 1-5 defeat at Crystal Palace, which was fairly symptomatic of the age for Cobblers fans. Carr wasn't dropped on this occasion, he simply shifted to No 4.

From a personal standpoint, I have always found it spooky that my first experience as a terrace Cobblers supporter on 27 April 1968 saw both Carr and Walker in the home ranks. Given that my destiny was to cover the club's fortunes in Northampton's evening paper, the *Chronicle & Echo*, for the first time during the record-breaking 1986-87 season, when Carr and Walker held the managerial and coaching reins, this was fitting.

Memories are sketchy of that baptism, shortly after my seventh birthday, but research shows that the Cobblers – then managed by Tony Marchi who had played as a wing-half during Spurs' famous double winning season of 1960-61 – drew 2-2 with Colchester United.

I remember the Hotel End fans singing 'relegation to you' to the small following from the Essex town, which represented a feat of opportunism since this was the only campaign, sandwiched into four drop years, when the Cobblers actually stayed up themselves.

While the Cobblers finished eighteenth that season, Colchester did indeed go down from Division Three in 23rd place. The U's finished above only Scunthorpe, which is where the astonishing team later assembled by Carr and coached by Walker began their momentous 1986-87 season under the eyes of my press-box scrutiny.

Goals by Glasgow-born John Byrne and Ron Flowers, who succeeded Marchi as player-manager for one season, cancelled out efforts by Colchester's Loughton and Price. Eighteen years later the outcome at Scunthorpe was again a 2-2 draw, although on that occasion the Cobblers spluttered after storming into a 2-0 lead in the first ten minutes with efforts from Richard Hill and Graham Reed.

Although the master-plan was in place, it was almost as though the side were still looking over their shoulder on that afternoon at The Old Show Ground, still expressing just a little self-doubt. So many years of comparative mediocrity – can we really go on and steamroller the rest of the division over the next eight and a half months?

The answer was simple that year. 'Of course we can'. Simply kick on and enjoy.

MARK BEESLEY

INTRODUCTION

Before the dawn, comes the darkest hour. In the case of Northampton Town, for all their troubled times during a turbulent 114-year history, there can be little doubt when the skies appeared at their most bleak and oppressive. The occasion was the Tuesday evening of 19 March 1985, when a crowd of just 942 witnessed a 0-2 home defeat by Chester City. The Ides of March might have passed by, but in the Cobblers' case it seems they were merely delayed a few days.

Chairman Neville Ronson had subconsciously decided that if ever there came a point when all the effort and heartache translated into gates below 1,000 paying spectators, then it was simply time to move on.

Negotiations with Kettering Town chairman John Murphy over a potential county merger with The Poppies fell flat at this time, and the ramifications of one short paragraph in the town's evening newspaper, the *Chronicle & Echo*, rumbled beneath the surface. It read simply: 'If you know of a suitable millionaire, just ring Northampton 31553 and ask for Nev Ronson.'

The seeds of disappointment for a dire campaign had been sown before a pre-season friendly at Shepshed Charterhouse, when newly appointed manager Tony Barton suffered a heart-attack. The hastily constructed team, under the charge of physio Richie Norman and former manager Clive Walker, was severely restricted in its preparations for what came next.

What actually came next was an opening day 0-5 thrashing at Exeter, a team which hardly set the world alight themselves that season in finishing eighteenth. It provided an omen for what followed. The Cobblers' only goal during their first eight matches (six league and a two-legged Milk Cup defeat by Crystal Palace) was a twice-taken penalty by Austin Hayes at home to Chesterfield, who went on to win the division by five points from Blackpool.

Herein lies another bitter irony. Hayes, in life a chirpy and effervescent character who won a Republic of Ireland cap in a 2-0 win over Denmark in 1979, and who played in Southampton's 2-3 League Cup final defeat that year by Nottingham Forest, died at the tender age of 29 in 1986, just three weeks after diagnosed with lung cancer.

It might have been significant that in the three-month period immediately preceding his death, Hayes had been playing in Sweden just after the nuclear disaster at Chernobyl in the Ukraine. Certainly, an uncommonly large number of cancer-related deaths were reported in northern Sweden that year.

It would be wrong, however, to write off season 1984-85 as a complete disaster. It is not as though there were not parallels with what had gone before. Only three years earlier the Cobblers failed to win any of their first dozen league matches and managed to end up 22nd in the table. That halcyon Division One campaign in 1965-66 failed to bring a victory in the first thirteen attempts before a win over West Ham. The other side of the coin had been 1983-84, when the club didn't lose any of their first eleven league games, yet still ended up in eighteenth place.

Goalkeeper Peter Gleasure was in his third season with the club and proved an admirable servant over a nine-year period while Ian Benjamin's eighteen league goals showed what a rare talent he truly was, in such an ineffective team. Both men experienced the Chester nadir (indeed they missed only five matches between them all season) and had good reason to weigh up the astonishing contrast which 1986-87 brought before them.

Warren Donald's late-season introduction, on loan from West Ham, provided another link with the championship era, as well as nudging a minor Cobblers miracle. After goals by Chester's Stuart Rimmer and Ricky Greenhough had sent Barton's men packing on that gloomy March evening, the headline in the next edition of the *Chronicle & Echo* screamed out: 'Can They Get Any Worse?'

Even here there was a thoughtful clue as to changing events, for as Keith Hursthouse's report observed: 'In a moment of supreme irony, Nuneaton boss Graham Carr – the man tipped to take the County Ground reins if Barton fails – came to offer words of consolation.'

After Chester, defeats at the hands of Scunthorpe and Crewe followed swiftly before a local derby trip to Peterborough on a Tuesday evening. The players could hardly have been inspired by the grim local paper headline, 'Escape Is Impossible!' which previewed the Posh trip, a confession from Barton that prospects of escaping the four places of the re-election zone that season were all but extinguished.

With nine matches remaining of this torpid campaign, the Cobblers sat nine points adrift of Rochdale and Wrexham at the foot of Division Four, and even a goalless draw in the Peterborough match hardly lifted the gloom. After all, it meant the club had not scored in their last six visits to London Road and had not won there since the 1972-73 season, when goals from John Hold and Graham Felton inspired a 2-1 victory. Thirteen games without a win, then, but while at the time it had seemed the Chester result meant the end of the line for Barton, he stayed in charge for another seven matches.

Barton was 47 when he had been appointed as Cobblers manager, but was no stranger to the County Ground, having played twice there for

Portsmouth in Division Two in the 1964-65 season, scoring in Pompey's 1-2 League Cup defeat and also turning out at outside-right in the memorable final match of Jimmy Dickinson's celebrated career. That 1-1 draw served to save Portsmouth from the drop, while also protecting the Cobblers' unbeaten home record in the final match of the season as they marched optimistically behind Newcastle into Division One.

Barton's playing career was spent with Fulham, Nottingham Forest and Portsmouth, where he also performed the task of player-coach. After managing Aston Villa to European Cup success against Bayern Munich, and the European Super Cup the next season, he joined the Cobblers before having a spell as assistant at Southampton under Chris Nicholl.

Barton might have been a gentleman himself but he was desperate to resurrect at least a semblance of the former glories he experienced at Villa Park. Yet, considering health issues and the resources placed at his disposal, he was placed in an almost impossible and certainly unenviable position at the finish. Perhaps he ought not to have chased the Cobblers' job in the first place — certainly there was a feeling among some of the Cobblers board they had been misled over health issues, and Barton died prematurely at the age of 56.

Both Barton and his young son Kieran were subject to abuse from frustrated home supporters, particularly during an early March 0-1 home Saturday defeat by Blackpool before a disastrous 0-4 thrashing at home by Wrexham three days later.

Expressing his commitment to the cause, Barton reported in his regular weekly column in the town's *Sports Pink*: 'We drink out of Northampton mugs at home and Kieran is proud to wear a Cobblers sweater.' Sadly, just as today, results on the field determine everything, with sensitivity thrown brutishly out of the window.

When the end came, it abounded with irony, arriving as it did on the back of three wins in four matches, coinciding with Barton winning a county-inspired initiative by Wellingborough firm Astraseal, as manager of the month for April — though he wasn't there for the last three games.

Whether Barton truly 'celebrated' his 48th birthday on 8 April 1985 must be a matter of conjecture, given the mood of the time, but the fact remains that 24 hours later the Cobblers soared to a first win in fourteen matches, thumping Stockport 4-0.

Donald opened the scoring with his first goal for the club, a rasping twenty-yarder, while a first league goal for Steve Brown, a man whose career highlight sixteen years later would be playing in an FA Cup semi-final for Wycombe Wanderers against Liverpool at Villa Park, prompted Benjamin and Aidy Mann to provide the others.

A 0-2 defeat at a resurrected Swindon followed, the Robins' being inspired by the reinstatement of boss Lou Macari a few days earlier. This left the Cobblers still seven points adrift of Wrexham at the foot of the table with seven games to play.

The next hectic run of four home fixtures proved nothing short of remarkable, split as they were between the management of Barton (against Hartlepool and Port Vale) and his successor, Carr (Tranmere and Darlington), yet providing a clean sweep of victories. You find yourself asking, where did that come from?

It struck me that, as the Cobblers had only won four home league games out of seventeen over a six-month span in 1984-85 prior to the Stockport victory, doubling that figure in an eight-day period showed a ridiculous high-speed turnaround in form.

Ronson had clearly made up his mind up about Barton, despite the sudden flurry of activity. On returning from a holiday in Minorca the Cobblers chairman severed the link, but not before Barton steered the Cobblers to a 2-0 win over Hartlepool on the Monday and a 1-0 success against Port Vale 48 hours later.

The Hartlepool match was remarkable for the fact that Donald scored with a screaming 40-yarder which flew into the top corner, beyond a despairing Eddie Blackburn (Brian Mundee getting the other goal), while none other than Brian Clough sat watching the club he first managed in the stands. Also in the directors' box that night was Carr, who had just won a Gola Manager of the Month award at Nuneaton.

Port Vale, a club local to Barton's Staffordshire home, were beaten with a Wakeley Gage goal which gave the Cobblers a first double in their fourth clash with the Potteries club that season, but Barton learned of his departure on arriving at the County Ground that afternoon and Carr was in charge for the visit of Tranmere.

Football is not life and death, whatever Bill Shankly might have said, and Barton's premature passing at the age of 56 in 1993 provided another sombre footnote to the era.

For followers of Northampton Town though, the wheel simply kept on turning with disrespectful haste in the immediate aftermath of Barton. 'Now Carr' snorted the headline in the *Chronicle & Echo*.

Goals by Benjamin and Brown gave Carr a winning start against Tranmere on the Saturday afternoon before Darlington, who had been promoted in third place behind Chesterfield and Blackpool, went down 1-2 on the Tuesday night, Donald setting up Benjamin for a last-gasp winner. Again, this combination proved a portent of better things soon to come.

Hereford were also vying for promotion but a Brown goal earned the Cobblers a 1-1 draw at Edgar Street on the Saturday and by the time Mansfield arrived for the club's ninth match in April, a new chairman had been unveiled.

Derek Banks, a Watford-based businessman dealing in tobacco, was half-Burmese and of Anglo-Indian parentage. He strode nonchalantly onto the County Ground pitch before the Stags' clash, raising his arms to acknowledge the cheers of the home faithful who were desperate to embrace a new Messiah.

If Banks seemed calm and in control of his emotions it was clearly just a well-disguised front, and one which lasted precisely nineteen minutes of the contest. For by the time Ray Train scored the only goal that night, the passion and love affair which sucks intelligent and otherwise passive individuals into the deep-seated traumas of a football club, causing them to part with all previous rationale, was already taking root.

Train strikes; Banks' interest rate rises. So much gloom and doom in the newspaper headlines for commuters and mortgage borrowers? No, simply the dawn of a new age at Northampton Town! For so it came to pass that the new man on board was the first to leap to his feet that night, and cheer what turned out to be the winner.

CHAPTER ONE

A Steering Job for Carr

As holidays go, the Carr family outing to Devon in the summer of 1985 did not turn out to be the special one it should have been. True, the new man at the helm had finally been given the chance to run the club where he had made 96 league and cup appearances as a player from his arrival as a raw sixteen-year-old in 1961, up until his departure in 1968, proving life truly did begin at 40.

Also, the jaunt to Torquay itself had something of a familiar ring about it (wasn't I here just a few weeks ago for a football match?). More significantly, however, a matter of pressing urgency was weighing on the mind of the Cobblers' new manager.

Carr had dealt with the end-of-season headache of releasing players he knew he needed to replace, if his master plan of transforming the club was to hold any substance. Gone were the likes of Michael Barnes, Ray Train, Paul Shirtliff, Paul Bancroft and Frankie Belfon, the striker who had entered Northampton folklore with two famous FA Cup goals in the 3-2 win over Gillingham in 1982-83 to earn a third-round tie with Tony Barton's Aston Villa, European champions.

Meanwhile, Carr also chose to part with Player of the Year Wakeley Gage, a popular Northampton-born figure of skyscraper proportions in the heart of defence, who set what was soon to become a fashionable trend by leaving the club on a high spot. He eventually signed for Harry McNally's Chester City after a summer of uncertainty.

Gage played for Chester against the Cobblers in a 2-2 draw at the County Ground in October and looked likely to return on a non-contract basis, only to be quickly offered a contract by Peterborough, where he continued to pop up on opposition team-sheets for some seasons to come.

The much-travelled Train, who departed for Tranmere, and Trevor Lee, whose eighth and final stop along the line was Fulham, both entered the category of seasoned pros who had playing careers to be proud of. Yet Carr's quest was to bring in younger, hungrier players who had a craving to succeed. And he had a good idea where to get them.

First though, he needed to be sure his new club would actually get a chance to challenge the likes of relegated Burnley and Preston, along with Hereford, Tranmere, and Colchester, who had just missed out on promotion the year before.

Despite ending the previous season with a rush of blood to the head and briefly moving out of the re-election zone on the final day – the 'impossible' task Barton had referred to just months before – subsequent points earned by Southend, Halifax and Stockport ensured that only one team eventually finished beneath the Cobblers – Torquay.

Carr's former club Nuneaton Borough had finished runners-up to Wealdstone in the Gola League in 1984-85, a position they had also occupied the previous season behind Maidstone, but it was fourth-placed Bath City who went forward as potential usurpers. Wealdstone's ground was deemed to be sub-standard.

While Bath's hopes seemed remote (they had even lost one match during the season, 0-6 at home to Kettering) there remained a doubt. It was still two more seasons before the champions of the top non-league tier could qualify for automatic promotion, provided their ground met the criteria, yet there was always the chance the Cobblers would not be voted back in by the Football League members.

The irony was not lost on Carr, who reflected: 'I still had it in the back of my mind that after finally getting a job in the Football League I could be straight out again, even after managing for five matches, and being unbeaten. I had a bad experience at Bradford Park Avenue, as I was there as a player for one season when they were voted out of the League in 1970 and replaced by Cambridge United after they had to apply for re-election for the fourth year running.

'That summer we had gone to Newquay on holiday with Terry Dolan and his family. Terry was with me that season at Bradford PA and later managed Bradford City and Rochdale. There was always talk about the 'old pals act' looking after the League clubs, but there were strong non-league clubs pushing to get in and we heard the news Bradford had been kicked out on the radio on the BBC Sports Report. It was a bit of a blow, to say the least.'

There was another Carr link with Torquay in the 1980s, as they had just appointed Stuart Morgan to try to turn around fortunes. Morgan had been one of Carr's close pals during his time at Weymouth, yet he said: 'I remember going back to Torquay on our family summer holiday in 1985 with Christine, Alan and Gary and not really enjoying it at all, with all of that League business hanging over me.'

In the event, the Cobblers comfortably survived the Football League's summer vote. The votes cast saw the Cobblers on top with 52, Stockport and Torquay earn 50, Halifax 48 and Bath City just eight.

Carr's career on the football ladder had in many ways been more dramatic than the Cobblers' own notorious 1960s rise and fall. He quipped:

'At least when Northampton dropped back to Division Four in 1969 they stopped – I kept going right down to the Southern League Premier.'

Always a wing-half, he had made his Cobblers debut as a player on 23 February 1963 in a 0-3 loss at Bournemouth, although it was another nine months before he had another chance – this time in a 3-2 home win over Middlesbrough. An uncompromising player, his reputation went before him. Latter-day football television pundits Jimmy Greaves and Ian St John both still claimed to carry the scars of opposition during the Cobblers' brief stay in Division One as they locked horns in combat for Tottenham Hotspur and Liverpool respectively. Both scored goals against Northampton that season, but Greaves' recollections likened Carr to 'an English equivalent of the American Football quarterback', backing up his analogy by adding: 'He used to tackle the man without the ball.'

Perhaps significantly, Carr used to admit that Graham Carr the player would never have survived under Graham Carr the manager – he knew all of the pitfalls, as he had his fair share of off-field scrapes.

From playing 27 times in Division One against the likes of the mighty Arsenal, Liverpool and Manchester United in 1965-66, Carr always laughed and said he knew 'something had gone wrong somewhere' with a disastrous four years that ended with Northampton back in Division Four by 1969, although he swapped the County Ground for York City's Bootham Crescent the summer before.

You would have thought a re-election campaign at York (21st place, ahead of just Newport, Grimsby and Bradford Park Avenue) could hardly get any worse, but by switching to Park Avenue for the 1969-70 campaign, Carr managed to drop another three rungs on the ladder as that club bombed out of the League from rock bottom, prompting a playing transfer to non-league.

Carr was never a goalscorer, failing to find the net for the first team during his time in Northampton's claret and white colours, but the habit slowly began to grow in him during his later days as a professional. His one and only goal for York arrived in a 4-0 win at Halifax on 11 January 1969 and in his final League season he managed to double that tally.

It seems that whatever more logical lessons Carr learned from his 1960s mentor, Dave Bowen, the art of goalscoring can also be included among them. During his time with Arsenal and the Cobblers, and his Welsh international career, Bowen only netted on four occasions: two of them in a north London derby at Tottenham, once for the Cobblers at Workington, and once representing his country in a World Cup qualifier in Tel Aviv against Israel. The lesson is to make them sparing and special occasions.

After being named Player of the Year in Bradford's last League season, Carr returned from a family holiday to find a letter on the mat informing him he had not been retained, so he joined Telford as captain, teaming up once more with ex-Cobblers manager Ron Flowers, in time for the 1970-71 season.

There he won an FA Trophy medal at Wembley after Telford beat a Hillingdon Borough side including ex-Cobbler Tommy Knox 3-2. Next stop along the line was Poole Town, before Carr won a Southern League Premier medal at Dartford, in a year when Northamptonshire neighbours Kettering Town were runners-up under Ron Atkinson. That season also included a second Wembley FA Trophy appearance, although Dartford lost in the final 1-2 to Morecambe.

Season 1974-75 saw Carr at Tonbridge's Angel Ground, but this time under the guidance of England 1966 World Cup legend George Cohen. The pair had opposed one another in Division One in the Cobblers' 4-1 win at Fulham's Craven Cottage in November 1965. After Tonbridge, there was still one more move as a player – the subsequent hop to Weymouth coinciding with a unique event for Carr: 'It was the first time any club paid money for me as a player although I think it was only £500,' he chuckled.

It was at Weymouth's Recreation Ground that the management bug took a convincing hold, players such as former England and West Brom centre-forward Jeff Astle coming under Carr's wing – indeed the pair ran a window-cleaning business together at the same time. However, it was the switch to manage Nuneaton in 1980 which brought matters on apace, with the Carr family taking the chance to move back to Northampton.

Five years at Nuneaton, five full seasons at Northampton – a relentless management tour, checking in with grasshopper-like hops, landing upon a range of destinations. Later spells in charge at Blackpool, Maidstone, Kettering and Weymouth for a second time seemed to confirm this wanderlust (or perhaps it is just part of the modern game culture), before ending in management at Dagenham & Redbridge, where Carr signed one of his old players, Graham Reed, for a third time.

No wonder the Carr football network proved so immense over a 35-year period, and led to an even more impressive 'CV' of scouting jobs, taking him all over the world. He graduated from a wing-half for such non-league satellites as The Dolphins of Poole Town to tackling such prominent 'network' positions for Coventry City, Tottenham Hotspur, Manchester City, Notts County and Newcastle United.

Locked in there have been some of the biggest names in the game: Gordon Strachan, George Graham and Glen Hoddle, Kevin Keegan,

Stuart Pearce, Sven Goran Eriksson, before Chris Hughton and Alan Pardew at St James' Park. Full circle, albeit a circle taken on a zig-zagging path which almost renders the M25 a perfect sphere. A wide, roundabout journey, which eventually led him home to the north-east for a lad originally brought up in the city on the Tyne.

The coincidences don't even stop there, as Carr pointed out: 'Newcastle's training ground on the Whitley Road in Benton is the area I grew up. You would think when I go up there and stay now that I would see more people there I knew, even after 50 years.'

Yet like most success stories, it took an age to happen. It needed the Northampton episode to prove Carr possessed qualities which stood him apart from the crowd. Qualities even recognised by such as the late Brian Clough, who famously shouted out 'Offside' when Carr went up to collect his Division Four Manager of the Year award in front of a packed arena in London in 1987.

Carr threw his hat into the ring for the Northampton post when Clive Walker stepped down in 1984: 'I first applied for the Northampton job when Tony Barton was given it before the 1984-85 season. Brian Barron from the *Chronicle & Echo* newspaper had rung me up and suggested I apply, and I dropped an application and CV in to Dave Bowen. To be fair, I never thought I had much chance against a man who had won the European Cup for Aston Villa against Bayern Munich two years earlier. In April 1985 Dave Bowen called me again and suggested I come to the ground for a meeting. When I arrived I remember seeing Neville Ronson's father Jack, and a young lad I later found out to be Derek Banks' son, kicking a ball about together in the corridor which led off from the board room. I then went in to meet Ronson and Banks. The following day, Dave Bowen went to see the Nuneaton chairman Noel Kelly and all of the arrangements for my appointment were ironed out.'

Carr always had a strategy in place, and Nuneaton were still to play a significant part in the shaping of that plan. For years he had been simply biding his time before landing the post he cherished, so much so that he took measures to keep his prized assets at Manor Park. 'Players such as Trevor Morley and Richard Hill were all on good contracts at Nuneaton as I didn't want to lose them.

'There was always a plan for Northampton. In my first of five years at Nuneaton, I had some success with old pros around me such as Tommy Robson, Roy Clayton the former Kettering striker, and Jon Sammels the old Arsenal and Leicester City player, and to be fair, they did exceptionally well for me. Yet I was in management by the age of 30 at Weymouth and I always had it in my mind about developing younger players who were hungry for the experience – at Nuneaton it meant recruiting the likes of Trevor Morley, Richard Hill and Eddie McGoldrick although I also signed the old Kettering Town striker and favourite Frankie Murphy. Eddie was playing at full-back for Kettering at the age of seventeen and I can't believe they let me sign both him and Frankie Murphy, if they had any sort of ambition at all.

'I always had it in my mind about the importance of using naturally left-footed players, which was where people such as Dave Gilbert came in. At Weymouth I had used two former Northampton players in Kevin Dove and Peter Hawkins, who played at outside-left at the County Ground in the early 1970s [1968-73] before they both went to Bedford.'

If the summer of 1985 was a fraught time for the manager, it was equally so for the players after that final-day success at Torquay, where goals by Russell Lewis and Ian Benjamin secured a 2-0 win. Ironically, they were men who would succeed local lad Gage as 'Player of the Year' over the next two seasons at Northampton before also then moving on. Goalkeeper Peter Gleasure bucked the trend by staying put for another four years, after being presented with this accolade in 1987-88.

In fact, Gleasure turned out to be a perennial survivor at Northampton for almost nine years, the benefits bringing a well-earned testimonial with Terry Venables' Tottenham at the County Ground in 1993, a contest watched by a crowd of over 2,000. This was some tribute, considering Gleasure had already left the County Ground fully a year by then.

At the end of his second full season, Gleasure survived the traditional end-of-season player cull in the week after the Torquay victory. The Gulls' location has historically provided plenty of fair-weather opportunity for Northampton teams and fans, Cobblers supporters being privileged to plan no fewer than eight May, August or September breaks on the English Riviera between 1978-2010 to coincide their passion for football with a top up of their sun tan.

If the notion of Torquay in May puts supporters in mind of an early chance for cream teas and sticks of rock, it was a different story for the Cobblers' hierarchy of 1984-85, which endured more disasters than an average half-hour episode of Fawlty Towers.

Hotels and pre-match meals had been off the agenda for players on away trips all season. Finance was so tight that they simply made do with a flask of coffee and sandwiches on the coach, and while this cash climate improved with the delivery of fresh investment from chairman Banks, there would inevitably be changes as Carr made room for new arrivals.

Gleasure had shipped 74 league goals in 1984-85 but Exeter and Southend fared worse, and while he was understandably nervous before being called into the manager's pokey dressing-room office, the result for him at least was a positive one.

'There was a really eerie feeling on that day, with the players sitting around and one by one being called into Graham's office,' Gleasure told me. While comparisons with the Roman emperor Caligula and the fallen gladiators in the arena are probably wide of the mark, he added: 'The players came out and either gave a "thumbs up" or "thumbs down" depending on whether they had been kept on or released.'

Carr took the view that Gleasure had done a fair job playing in a moderate team, without having the best protection in front of him. The fact that the goalkeeper eventually spent more than eight seasons with the club, from 1983-1991, bore testament to that fact. Gleasure made 344 league appearances, a further tribute to his durability. He also kept a club record of 112 clean sheets in a full total of 412 matches.

At different stages along the line, challengers such as Tim Garner, Kevin Poole, Alan Harris and Marlon Beresford popped up in his wing mirror (Gleasure has been a driving instructor since hanging up his boots, after a brief spell on loan to Gillingham and Hitchin Town), only to disappear from view. Beresford ultimately succeeded him but Gleasure enjoyed five complete ever-present seasons with Northampton, as well as two others where he missed three games or less.

The Luton-born shot-stopper had arrived on loan from Millwall in March 1983, making his debut in a 2-1 home win over Scunthorpe. His career at The Den saw him make 55 appearances from 1980-82. There, he was a member of the Lions' successful FA Youth Cup-winning team in 1979 when they defeated Manchester City 2-0 over two legs, drawing 0-0 away and winning 2-0 at home.

Gleasure's team-mates at that time included future Ipswich Town and Republic of Ireland internationals Kevin O'Callaghan and Tony Kinsella, along with Phil Coleman and Paul Roberts, who went on to play for Colchester and Southend. Goalkeeper Alex Williams and Tommy Caton were among the City team. Gleasure noted: 'We beat Nottingham Forest in the quarter-finals and Everton in the semis. I remember Brian Clough coming into our dressing room to congratulate us after the Forest win.'

Gleasure's Millwall days were numbered when George Graham replaced Peter Anderson in 1982, Graham arriving with former Cobblers skipper and future manager Theo Foley as assistant. Gleasure said: 'It was obvious from the start that Graham didn't really like me. Mind you, I wasn't that keen on him myself.' I was given the chance to come on loan to

Northampton and it seemed a sensible move for me as I was a Luton lad anyway.'

There were mixed fortunes for Gleasure at Millwall, where he shared goalkeeping duties with Paul Sansome and Peter Wells. On one occasion he found himself on the opposing side to future Cobblers' team-mate Phil Cavener in a match Burnley won 5-0 at Turf Moor in September 1980. Yet with his nose put out of joint by Graham at Millwall, at least Gleasure didn't feature in front of the *Match of the Day* cameras when Huddersfield thrashed Millwall 5-1 in Division Three during 1982-83, nor for the earlier 0-1 FA Cup defeat at Slough that season.

Turf Moor again became an early-season focus for Gleasure and Cavener for the Cobblers at the onset of 1985-86. The goalkeeper was one of just five players who started the final game of 1984-85 at Torquay and the opener for the next campaign at Burnley, almost three and a half months later. Assured of a place in the '92 club' once more, Carr wasted precious little time in moving matters on.

The other survivors from Torquay were Brian Mundee, Russell Lewis, Aidy Mann and Ian Benjamin, although Cavener returned after a near six-month injury lay-off against his old club, while Warren Donald's return to West Ham after the expiry of his loan period was to prove only a temporary departure.

Debuts came for Paul Curtis from Charlton and Ian Dawes from Newcastle, as well as Richard Hill and Trevor Morley from Nuneaton, and Graham Reed from Frickley. It was the latter pair – Morley and Reed – who found their way onto the scoresheet on the opening day in a 2-3 defeat by the pre-season favourites. Burnley were playing in the bottom section for the first time in their 103-year history and the crowd of 4,279 would be the largest to watch the Cobblers in an away league fixture that season.

With all due respect to right-back Curtis and young centre-half Dawes – who was attempting to find fortune and follow in the manager's own playing footsteps some 35 years earlier by moving south from Newcastle – it was soon apparent that the likes of Morley, Hill and Reed would make the quickest and most significant impressions.

Mind you, chairman Banks' horror to learn that many Cobblers fans were placing their hard-earned cash on the side getting promotion on what would essentially be a learning curve year, seemed fully justified at half-time at Turf Moor on 17 August with Carr's men 0-3 down.

Burnley included Alan Taylor, the man who had scored both West Ham goals in the 2-0 win over Fulham in the 1975 FA Cup final, yet the first-half damage was done by Kevin Hird, Wayne Biggins and a Mundee own-goal, the full-back volleying spectacularly into his own net after Biggins had cannoned a rebound at him following a corner.

It was too early to despair as the Cobblers' players trooped off towards the tunnel behind the goal, but Reed, used in attack alongside Morley, recalled: 'The manager slaughtered us one by one at half-time but I remember saying that Trevor and I hardly had a kick up front.'

Matters improved considerably after the break, with Cavener sending Morley clear in the 48th minute, allowing the new Cobblers skipper to chip goalkeeper Joe Neenan for his first goal for the club, while Reed made it 2-3 four minutes from time when he latched onto Aidy Mann's pass to spear a shot under the goalkeeper.

However, Reed still recalls missing a great chance in the dying moments to equalise, volleying over from three yards. It all seemed to justify Banks' reaction as he cringed afterwards: 'Give us time – we are looking to finish in the top half of the table.'

In many ways, the performance summed up the mood of 'rehearsal season' for what was to follow. Enormous strides had clearly been made from the catalogue of disasters in 1984-85, with no shortage of promise potential, goals and entertainment. However, there was still something 'half-built' or flawed in the smooth running of the machine. The nature of it was all the more enthralling for its being so unpredictable.

The Burnley match was one of seven in league and cup to end in enterprising 3-2 finishes, yet only one ended in victory, that coming perversely enough at Chester, who were to finish runners-up to Swindon, after losing only three times at home all season.

One of the preambles penned by *Chronicle & Echo* reporter Keith Hursthouse pointed out that that Carr's men had a tough start to the season, with matches at Burnley, Swindon and at home to Preston among the first five. Perhaps predictably, given the information already supplied, those away games were both lost 2-3, while Preston were buried 6-0 at the County Ground!

Excitement also reached fever pitch with a delicious 5-0 local derby win at Peterborough, a 4-0 Friday night win at Southend – which arrived thirteen days after a victory by the same margin at home to Halifax in late November. Sandwiched in between was a 5-2 win at Cambridge United's Abbey Stadium, so thirteen of that season's 79 league goals arrived in three consecutive matches.

Some of the victories were immense and a statistician's dream. This was proven by the fact that 1985-86 remains one of only three seasons in the Cobblers' league history that they have won matches by 6-0, 5-0, 4-0, 3-0, 2-0 and 1-0 margins. It also happened in 1951-52 and again 24 years later when Bill Dodgin's Division Four promotion crew provided a memorable County Ground highlight with a 6-0 home blitz of Bournemouth, all the goals arriving in the first half.

That was during an age when Gerry Harrison presented the Anglia *Match of the Week* programme and Cobblers' fans were able to enjoy the sequence again after their Sunday lunchtime roasts, 24 hours later. Pity though, *Chronicle & Echo* photographer Bob Price, who chose that of all afternoons to sit behind the home goal in the first half, by way of a change. By the time he had reverted to type in the second half it was all too late, and even an attempt to capture the action by snapping at his television screen on Sunday failed to bring the quality required for reproduction in Monday evening's paper.

Yes, 1985-86 was truly the 'Countdown' season, although the side ultimately ended in eighth place, a respectful fifteen points behind the last of the promoted sides, Port Vale, and never at any stage held a position which suggested promotion was likely.

It all appears with hindsight to have been a carefully orchestrated preparation for the mighty blast off which would take place the following year. 'Countdown.'

At moments like these I like to hark back to my childhood, and puppet tales of 'International Rescue' on the television in the late 1960s and all those wonderful rockets waiting patiently on the launch pad. It was during an era when I also penned a Weekend Diary on a Monday morning at Kingsthorpe Church of England junior school, written almost exclusively (it seems now) about football.

I still laugh when I remember one of the first literal errors to blot my copybook referred to York City's Paul Aimson opening the scoring at the County Ground after eight minutes, scoring from an acute 'angel'. This was also the time of a generally forgotten British sci-film movie named *Thunderbird Six*.

So let your minds wander. Never mind Gerry Harrison and *Match of the Week* (for this popular Sunday afternoon programme went off the air in 1983), cue Gerry and Sylvia Anderson instead, and the theme music from *Thunderbirds* at a time when I still donned short trousers (even off the football field) as the credits roll and we prepare to pay tribute to the Countdown Season some years on, in 1985-86.

Kicking off against Preston on a Tuesday night in early September, I can imagine the engine roar of Scott Tracy piloting Thunderbird One on the rocket launch-pad as the seconds tick away to blast-off:

6-0! Richard Hill scores a hat-trick as the once proud Lancashire giants of Preston are proud no longer.

5-0! Peterborough 0, Northampton 5. This is what happens to the old enemy when their goalkeeper John Turner is sent off by referee David Axcell after only six minutes.

4-0! Quite a surreal Friday night in Essex as Schiavi and Curtis are among the December goalscorers at Southend.

3-0! Benjamin (two) and Hill are on the scoresheet as Hartlepool are sent packing at the County Ground.

2-0! Revenge has been exacted on Burnley for that opening-day defeat. How dared they!

1-0! So good they named it twice, with back-to-back wins over Colchester and Orient at the end of March.

0-0! A popular Northampton philosophy is that if you are going to end the season on a stalemate, you might as well spoil a promotion party at Port Vale (Northampton also won 2-1 there on the final day of 1982-83 when Vale were celebrating promotion). Being present at promotion parties in advance is also useful to lend a few ideas for next season. It was probably a case of 'crack open the Port Vale'. So, take a deep breath and get ready for lift-off. Thunderbirds are go!

The more attentive of you will realise that the countdown sequence is not portrayed in a totally chronological sequence. Frustrating that! The Preston drubbing set the ball rolling on 10 September, while Peterborough were clobbered on 12 October. Halifax (23 November) and Southend (6 December) provided the 4-0 double but we had to wait until 11 March for the 3-0 win over Hartlepool, by which time the season's brace of 2-0 successes at Colchester (26 October) and at home to Burnley (18 January) had been recorded. I suppose 1-0s are relatively common (five of those) with the last two (Colchester at home and Orient away) sitting back-to-back in March. What we really needed was a second goal in the home match against Colchester to make it all fit in. I shall have a word with Hilly boy about missing that sitter the next time I see him.

On a more serious note, 1985-86 was also the first season after the fire disaster at Bradford City in May 1985 which claimed 56 lives. While there were obvious ramifications on a wider scale, the effect at Northampton was in its own way dramatic. Former team manager, then general manager and club secretary Dave Bowen came out in the local press with a classic 'Our ground is worse than Bradford' quote on the Monday after the Bradford fire – which in fairness it almost certainly was. People had been making offensive remarks about the ramshackle home which doubled as a cricket ground for years. Certainly in the mid-1960s in Division One it stuck out like a sore thumb when Manchester United, Arsenal and Liverpool were among the visitors.

Bowen and Carr had visited Valley Parade three weeks before the Bradford fire to watch a reserve match which featured a young Paul Gascoigne playing for Newcastle, so they knew at first hand the tinder-box scenario and the difficulties of escape along the rows to the exits.

Bowen almost certainly hoped to use the Bradford terror as a lever to finally persuade Northampton's council to take positive steps towards providing the club with a new stadium (in fact, it would take another nine years) but the immediate effect was the condemnation of the wooden upper seating in the old main stand on Abington Avenue, directly opposite the side shared with the county cricket ground, where supporters had stood for years on the duck boards during the winter.

Having frequented those wooden boards as a young fan, memorably during the Bill Dodgin 1975-76 promotion year when the side finished second behind Graham Taylor's Lincoln City, I can confirm that the close-up contact with the players sometimes gave the whole place the air of a Sunday morning on the local park, despite at that time having a packed main stand opposite.

While the hastily constructed 'Meccano Stand' eventually provided some seating recompense for directors, season-ticket holders and press alike, it wasn't opened until the 1 March win over Rochdale in 1986, and for a testing spell, assembled home and away scribes and radio reporters were banished to the far yonder.

On 14 December 1985 I was present for the Cobblers v Port Vale fixture in my capacity as a sidekick to former *Chronicle & Echo* and *London Evening Standard* journalist John Morris, who was to become Secretary of the British Boxing Board of Control the following May.

No great surprises there, as this was a task I had regularly and willingly undertaken since joining the town's weekly *Northants Post* newspaper eighteen months earlier, but the difference on this occasion was that we were seated in the enclosed and elevated cricket press-box more than 200 yards away from the action. Armed with a pair of antiquated binoculars, which I believe had last seen service during Montgomery's campaign against Rommel at El Alamein in north Africa during the Second World War, I settled down for an afternoon of surreal entertainment.

Largely due to more collusion and discussion than you witness on an average heat of *University Challenge*, press colleagues were in full agreement that Phil Sproson had headed home Paul Maguire's free-kick in first-half stoppage time, and that Morley had turned on a sixpence to equalise 21 minutes from the end.

Unity was also fulsome in the praise for Robbie Earle's 77th-minute right-foot drive which restored Vale's advantage, but one thing you didn't want under the glow of the County Ground floodlights in mid-December was a goalmouth scramble from a corner-kick four minutes from time, which led to an equaliser.

Eight or so confused and flagging football writers and broadcasters with deadlines looming, turned to one another in various bewildering states to ask the natural question: 'Exactly who had followed up to score, after Hill's header had come back from the crossbar?'. A variety of 'I don't know', 'search me' and 'haven't a clue pal' were among the more enlightening responses.

Ah, at least, a practical solution to the dilemma from my mentor, Mr Morris. 'Actually Mark, would you mind popping down and finding out?' Nothing beats a willing volunteer.

One of the few good things about the County Ground's unique geography over the years was that football patrons in need of a bracing stroll either side of the cricket square could avoid the untimely queues on the final whistle and at least retrace David Capel's summer run-up by heading for the Wantage Road exit several minutes early.

So after clambering down three flights of stairs and charging in the gloom towards the still vibrant Hotel End, I met the first of the homeward bound supporters. They were now more focused on their mug of Bovril and whether the Cobblers' late spoiler had brought them eight draws with Vernons Pools by tuning into James Alexander Gordon on their radio. Surely they would want to know who had scored the damn thing – if only to buy the culprit a pint.

After a couple of pretty dumb responses, the 'safety in numbers' theory began to pan out. 'I think it was Chard', 'number 4,' 'Chard mate.' I quickly worked out this wasn't the occasion for graphic detail and turned on my heels to head back to the cricket watchtower, where happily the name Phil Chard was recorded as the scorer of the Cobblers' equaliser.

The farcical cricket press-box coverage went on for some time, even though Morris managed to persuade the powers that be that a small standing area above the dug-outs should be made available for press before the Meccano stand – so called as it was easily assembled and probably came in a box with fitting instructions – was ready. However, the binocular operation certainly captured the wider imagination, although Morris recalled: 'I remember my old 1950s colleague Maurice Ribbans standing on the duck boards with an early prototype of the mobile phone which was a massive thing.

Season 1985-86 involved a great supporting cast of characters, which included *Coronation Street*'s Johnny Briggs and future England World Cup hero David Platt, as well as the more obvious ones closer to home. It was the campaign when Northampton Town photographer Pete Norton began an association of snapping away at the club which spans an unbroken 26 years.

The sort of humour presumably passed on to Carr's eldest son, Alan, to enable him to become one of the country's most prominent cult comedians during the aptly named 'Noughties' was, it seems, passed on to his Northampton players. The kidnapping attempt of *Coronation Street* actor Johnny Briggs, who played Mike Baldwin for many years, is a case in point.

National headlines were avoided, as it never quite came off, but the fact remains that Briggs ended up on the team coach after a 'let your hair down' night at the White Swan at Bucklow Hill in Cheshire amid loud terrace-like chanting, so it might easily have done.

It hadn't exactly started out as a February night of celebration – the Cobblers had just been beaten 0-1 at Stockport, and Carr's frustrated sense of annoyance needed working upon. 'I wasn't going to stop on the way home but Clive [Walker] told me not to be so silly and we decided to all have a drink. I think Dick Underwood gave Trevor Morley £50 to put behind the bar for everyone, which was a lot of money in those days, and it all took off from there.'

Some of the antics are probably not repeatable in a family publication, but Briggs had clearly enjoyed a good night himself in the White Swan and played the part of a willing co-respondent. At one point it looked as though he would be carted off back south on the M6, as some sort of celebrity treasure to be paraded at home to Rochdale the following week. He could even have cut a white ribbon and opened the Meccano Stand.

Platt and scarcely less well-known future England international Geoff Thomas were both more-or-less regulars in Crewe v Northampton fixtures over several seasons. In 1984-85 both played and Platt was on the scoresheet in Crewe's 3-1 win at the County Ground, although he did not appear in the earlier game at Gresty Road when Thomas scored in a 3-2 victory.

The next season, Platt was involved in both Cobblers matches, but Thomas in only the Cobblers' 1-0 win at Gresty Road, which came courtesy of a Morley goal. The early season 0-1 defeat at the County Ground was a classic example of an 'After The Lord Mayor's Show' performance, coming as it did four days after the walloping of Preston.

Platt went on to win 62 England caps and is best remembered for his wonder strike against Belgium in Italia 1990 which booked a quarter-final place against Cameroon, but in 1986-87 he and his Crewe team-mates could find no answers to the hat-trick magic of Hill in the Cobblers' 5-0 demolition at Gresty Road, when The Railwaymen were shunted into the sidings in no uncertain manner. Thomas missed that, but both played in the April 1987 return on a memorable night when the Cobblers clinched the divisional title.

The slightly tenuous footnote to the Platt/Cobblers link actually concerned Italia 90, when Graham Reed and Russell Wilcox witnessed the victory in Bologna. Reed recalled: 'We travelled from Milan on a train and I remember standing on the platform at Turin when we suddenly heard fans chanting "Rambo, Rambo". Russ and the guys with us couldn't believe it.'

The tough-man nickname was one which Reed happily bore during his Cobblers' career, and the County Ground faithful weren't going to let him forget it just two years after he had left the club, initially signing for VS Rugby. Who says Northampton Town supporters are an insular breed?

Norton's life as a postman and as a local park referee was never going to be the same once his keen interest in photography had attached itself limpet-like to the Cobblers. His first away game was the Peterborough Milk Cup-tie which ended in a 0-0 draw on 21 August 1985 (the Cobblers booking a second round two-legged tie with Division One Oxford after winning the return 2-0) while a first league outing on the road followed at Rochdale (a 2-3 defeat) a month later.

Northampton matches that Norton has missed since are few and far between, probably no more than a dozen in total in 26 years, and probably not worth knowing about. Yet he still remembers a rare absence from a 0-1 home defeat by Fulham in October 1996, when his daughter Jennifer was born:

'My wife Bernie was at her mum's and I was all ready to go the match at 12 o'clock when I had a phone call saying I had better get down to the hospital. I said to one of the nurses I was sure the baby would be a girl as no boy would be born on a match day, and sure enough that's how it turned out.

'My son Alex was born after a cup defeat at Reading in a night match in August 1993. He was overdue, yet I was still able to deliver photographs to the papers at Kettering and Northampton between 2-3am that night before he arrived at 4pm the next day. The funniest thing there was asking a guy in the hospital car-park for change for the meter. I saw him again half-an-hour later when I found out he was the gynaecologist delivering the baby.'

This wasn't a memorable season for Cup exploits, the FA Cup ending in the first round with a 0-3 exit at Gillingham, while Oxford duly carried out their expected execution in the second round of the Milk Cup by a 4-1 aggregate (2-1 at home and 2-0 at the County Ground). The Freight Rover Trophy run ended with a 2-3 defeat at Bristol City in the southern quarter-final after earlier wins over the Essex pair, Colchester and Southend.

If there is a clue as to what would follow the next season, nine victories on the road probably provide it. Morley's classic strike which rounded off the 5-2 romp at Cambridge United in November was a high spot. Despite languishing only eleventh in the table after this success, the Cobblers were then the division's highest scorers with 44 goals from twenty matches.

A 2-0 victory in a morning kick-off at Colchester also stands out, although the aftermath brought a car crash which ultimately hastened the end of the playing career of ex-Northampton striker Keith Bowen, son of club legend Dave.

A magical 60 seconds at high fliers Chester in February, the Cobblers coming from two goals down after sixteen minutes to earn an unlikely victory, was also remarkable. Hill headed in a Mann cross seven minutes before the break before Schiavi (72) and Morley (73) completed the transformation.

However, the next four away games were lost (Stockport, Wrexham, Hereford and Scunthorpe) without even a goal scored and, despite successes at Orient (1-0) and Tranmere (3-1), the season ended on a downward spiral.

Perhaps at times the team spirit was almost too good. Certainly the post-match eating and drinking habits would have been questionable today, but then the game has changed immeasurably.

Carr said: 'I used to think it was good to stop for a drink on the way home as it kept the team camaraderie going. It allowed players to get things off their chests if they had a problem. It's a bit different from today where they have dieticians on the team coach. In those days we used to know where all the take-away shops were, the one at Tranmere springs to mind.'

Only one win in the final seven matches after Tranmere buried any lingering chance of promotion in Carr's first full season. I can't help wondering whether, despite those goals from Benjamin, Stewart Hamill and Paul Sugrue, the Prenton Park take-away should just have been restricted to grabbing the points, and not fuelling up on extra batter bits.

Hamill and Sugrue were only 'passing through' performers, but the former at least established a small niche in Northampton folklore. Not many Cobblers players have counted their previous Highland League clubs as Anniesland, Possill and Pollock in Scotland, although Billy Best came from Pollock.

Carr knew of Hamill, having signed him as a loan player at Nuneaton, but can't have expected his immediate impact. Despite making only three league starts, the wide-man notched a goal in the ninth minute of the Freight Rover defeat at Bristol City, but trumped that at Tranmere by opening the scoring inside 60 seconds.

The seven-match run-in was in many ways a bizarre one, again forming a fair impression of a spluttering Rolls Royce engine which is just defective in the odd part.

Carr's men began it by roaring into a 2-0 lead against Exeter inside the first eight minutes, only to be held 2-2, ultimately by a Paul Friar own-goal thirteen minutes from time.

Leads were also then tossed away at home to Aldershot (2-3) and Leyton Orient (2-3), with future Cobbler Bobby Barnes scoring twice in the first one, while the O's Alan Comfort scored one and made a goal in the Londoners' success.

No doubt the odd prayer has also been quietly offered for Cobblers fans who ever look back and remember the 0-2 defeat at Halifax which followed. Both goals were scored by Dave Longhurst, the Corby lad who returned to his native county to play for the Cobblers in 1987, only to tragically die of a heart attack on the pitch in September 1990 when playing in a match for York City against Lincoln.

The return of Brian Mundee to the County Ground just seven weeks after signing for Cambridge brought a sense of inevitability when he fired into the Hotel End goal during Cambridge's 2-0 victory on 26 April. For County Ground fans, Hill redressed the balance three days later by scoring his first Cobblers hat-trick in a 5-1 win over Torquay, a result which again condemned The Gulls to bottom spot in Division Four.

If the mention of Torquay United in late April brought with it a sense of the familiar, so did the season's swansong at Port Vale, acting as party-poopers once more. What happened next, though, would be slightly less predictable.

CHAPTER TWO

The Watford Connection (I)

Selected train stations dotted along the West Coast main line of Britain's rail network held special significance to supporters of Northampton Town and beyond during the football season of 1986-87. Not all of them perhaps, but a surprising percentage.

Glasgow, and the most northern English outpost of Carlisle, were admittedly some way off the radar (like the passing of two high speed locomotives, The Cumbrians were relegated from Division Three, so missing the chance of meeting up for another four years). A little further south, Lancaster had some relevance to Northampton Town's fortunes years earlier, for it was from here that chairman Banks' predecessor, Neville Ronson, had moved in his early childhood to provide a crucial link in the chain of the club's history.

Another red herring proved to be Milton Keynes. Such can be the intransigence of Northampton folk that you're better not to discuss development around Milton Keynes Central around the old shoe town, as it remains something of a sore point.

However, you could dip in at Preston, Crewe, Nuneaton, Rugby and Northampton's Castle Station itself, before arriving at Watford Junction, to find people quite frankly all 'talking Cobblers', regardless of whether their particular kinship was of a claret and white persuasion.

The mention of Preston and Crewe triggers significant Division Four opposition in 1986-87. Preston (or should that be Pressed-On in both the Cobblers and the Lancashire club's case?) gave sporting chase to the Cobblers' runaway express to ensure any complacency was kept largely at bay.

As well as being the venue for the finest home-made fish cakes on the lower league circuit (if only I'd got there to sample them!), a match with Crewe was to provide the ultimate crowning glory night. Nuneaton and Watford helped to provide the tools to get the job done, while Northampton's very own Castle Station speaks loudly for itself.

Kinship or kingship? It's hard to say in a town which swapped sides and aligned with the Roundheads in the Civil War back in the seventeenth century. That's why we don't have a castle any more, only a station. When Charles II took a dim view of the town's loyalties on restoring the Royalists' Stuart line back on the throne in 1660, he made quite sure of that.

Yet rarely since the occasion when Archbishop Thomas Becket appeared before Henry II's council at Northampton Castle in 1164, had the town felt so central to any national plot, let alone a main line theme (Northampton's railway station is actually on a west-coast loop, as if something of a planning afterthought which will strike a familiar chord to many of the town's brethren). For once though, the Cobblers were indeed to prove kings of the castle in 1986-87 and put the town firmly on the map in a mighty football campaign.

I offer no apology for indicating the Rugby connection. Terry Branston, a wonderful whole-hearted character and team-mate warrior from Carr's Division One days, was Rugby through and through, living there while a player with Northampton, Lincoln and Luton. He sat regularly behind me in the hastily erected Meccano Stand with his old pal and Cobblers director Don Hammond as the wonderful 1986-87 campaign unfolded, and was always sharp with his assessments. Had he borrowed Carr's contacts' list and had the inclination, I've no doubt he would have proved a worthwhile television pundit.

At the book launch of *Northampton Town: A Season in the Sun 1965-66*, Branston proved a life and soul of the party. Sadly, he passed away during the creation of this current offering and over 500 people crammed St Andrews' Church in Rugby for the service. However, there remains another curious fact which tells you everything you need to know about Northampton thinking, and which goes back to the spirit of '86.

On Monday, 13 October 1986 the club finally got around to giving Branston a testimonial match. Bear in mind this is almost twenty years after he left the club and you have some idea about the speed and purpose of Northampton thinking, particularly when slanted to planned stadium projects. Incidentally, referee Ken Baker who took charge of the testimonial night became the Rev Ken Baker for the funeral service.

Back on the railway track theme, the Cobblers had been getting derailed at Gresty Road for years prior to Morley's 1985 strike which earned a 1-0 win, only one point earned during six visits in consecutive seasons from 1979-1984. So much so, that the *Sports Pink* headline: 'No change for Cobblers at Crewe,' on a Saturday evening became something of a standing dish, despite the groans which invariably greeted it when the newspaper started to hit the town shops from around 5.30pm.

So what could be finer than to reserve one of your most stunning performances of the season in the railway town before clinching the title in the return leg five months later? 'All change at Crewe,' or 'Crewe cut down to size' helped suddenly breathe a semblance of freshness and originality to the proceedings.

Until Northampton won 3-0 at Preston in 1995-96 with a Neil Grayson hat-trick, the club had never tasted success in eleven league visits in what appeared to be darkest and most remote Lancashire when it came to the quest for league points. While the most commonly retained fact about the Cobblers as a football club is their 2-8 defeat by a George Best-inspired Manchester United in the FA Cup during 1969-70, Deepdale was also the venue for their exit on their only other excursion to the fifth round of this competition, in 1933-34. On this occasion the score-line was only 0-4.

Clearly, there were a few old scores to settle here, although the Cobblers' first venture onto a plastic surface in April 1987 did not reap the hoped-for revenge, even if it did produce the biggest Division Four audience for over five years. A crowd of 16,456 saw Town lose 0-1, and while that in no way compared to the 25,593 who had seen Sheffield United draw 1-1 with Bradford City at Bramall Lane, it was further evidence that football at the lowest professional tier could both excite and flourish.

However, short of relegating Manchester United into Division Four for one season to satisfy your thirst (unlikely), surely a championship clinched by nine points, with The Lilywhites trailing in your wake, is as close to heaven as you will get, with perhaps local rivals Peterborough United back in third? Notice that our mind-set is not so bitter and twisted as to want to get The Posh relegated. It is worth considering that had they been well enough equipped to earn promotion behind us, Carr's men could have had the satisfaction of beating them home and away again the following season as well.

I always remember the Cobblers' secretary Dr John Evans (the other non-playing member to join the club from Nuneaton), expanding on his West Bromwich Albion v Wolverhampton Wanderers supporters' theory. Speaking as an ardent Baggies fan (he went on to be secretary at The Hawthorns for many years), Dr Evans explained it was a hopeless situation to have the Old Gold shirts slumming it down in Division Four as happened at this time. How could you sustain a rivalry with a club if you never played them? Thankfully for advocates of the Dr Evans theory, Wolves were the next Division Four champions in 1987-88.

One didn't need to buy a west-coast main-line ticket to Northampton to learn of the club's sudden Lazarus-like recovery under Carr. Quite simply, the Cobblers' achievements and manner of attaining them in 1986-87 earned acclaim in football circles and column inches in the national press, while television crews again checked out railway links and East Midlands approach roads. It was like a rebirth.

In the *Daily Express*, John Wragg wrote in October 1986: 'It is so hard finding your way round Northampton's ground, you can understand why the club has been lost in the Fourth Division for nearly 10 years. Half the place is a cricket ground, the football end didn't have a proper stand until recently and the offices are across the road, in what used to be a terraced house.'

Use your imagination a little, and it was possible to conjure up another express ride to the very top, although those more savvy individuals familiar with the town would have been shrewd enough to invest in a return ticket.

How ironic that for rail purposes, Northampton should locate somewhere like a midpoint stop between Nuneaton to the north and Watford heading south. The two towns might not noticeably have much in common (actually Nuneaton shocked Watford 3-0 in a first round FA Cup-tie in 1953), but the impact of a clutch of their former players and manager on the one hand, and an enthusiastic, football-loving businessman on the other, resulted in a pincer movement which brought a devastating effect. In both cases, light the blue touch paper while standing 50 miles or so away. Eventually it will lead to the County Ground where the Cobblers will be set alight.

While Carr had the players and the management nous, Banks threw in enough capital to make a small explosion. 'How much do you need to get us promotion?' Banks asked Carr on one of the pair's first ever meetings. '£40,000,' came the reply. 'Then you can have £60,000,' Banks instantly responded. Years later he reflected: 'Even then he didn't spend it all at once.'

If Nuneaton was the magical chest from which Carr and the Cobblers reaped a rich store of golden nuggets, then the Watford connection undoubtedly provided the key to unlocking it.

Taking the rail analogy a step (or station) further down the line, regular train commuters will know that once you leave Watford, it is not long before you are swallowed up by a mass of depressing London tenement blocks. Yet before you disappear into the darkest of tunnels, the twin towers of Wembley loom up somewhere on your left to offer a symbol of hope. It was here in 1984 that the dream was born for tobacco businessman Banks, and his schoolboy chum Mike Conroy.

The pair had been friends since their days together at St James High School in Burnt Oak, near Edgware, and continued into early adult life when Banks' aspirations of taking off were probably nurtured by six years spent in the RAF. Following Watford up from Division Three under the management of Graham Taylor and the inspiring chairman status of

Elton John (he held that position from 1976 until 2002) became a welcome distraction for the pair.

The timing of Taylor's own start in management was perversely due in part to the Cobblers, as he was seriously injured in a Division Four match in February 1972 at the County Ground which Lincoln won 3-2. Although he attempted a comeback the following season, it was not successful, which allowed him to turn thoughts more seriously to management, taking over from David Herd in December 1972. In getting the post at Sincil Bank he became the youngest ever manager in the Football League at 28 and narrowly pipped Carr's former Cobblers playing colleague, the aforementioned and now lamented Branston to the post.

Taylor's talent as a football boss quickly became apparent as the Cobblers found to their cost, forced, as Bill Dodgin's side were, to cede the Division Four championship to The Imps by six points in 1975-76. Taylor then succeeded Mike Keen at Watford in 1977 as his career began to blossom. Again there was a Cobblers twist, for Keen's next job in management was at the County Ground, where he took over from Johnny Petts for a year.

After Watford won the Division Four title in 1977-78 by eleven points from Southend, Banks and Conroy followed the Hornets' fortunes up into Division One, which they reached in 1982. It represented a dramatic rise in fortunes, on a par with the Cobblers' own meteoric rise to Division One in 1965-66, the sort of feat which could easily inspire 'Cinderella' style ambitions.

Watford made a fair fist of that and finished runners-up to Liverpool in Division One in 1982-83, to leave Banks recalling: 'Mike Conroy and I were at the FA Cup final in 1984 when Watford were beaten 0-2 by Everton, and also at the club's first European match that season when they defeated Kaiserslautern 3-0 after losing the first leg 1-3 away.' After beating Levski Spartak 4-2 on aggregate, Watford bowed out in the third round to Sparta Prague 2-7 on aggregate. Still, who would have seen that one coming ten years earlier?

With tireless monotony it seems, there is once more a Northampton-Watford link in both that FA Cup final and the Kaiserslautern UEFA Cup-tie. Lining up in the Watford team at Wembley was the beanpole ex-Corby Town striker George Reilly, who scored 45 goals for the Cobblers from 1976-79, at which point he moved to Cambridge.

Against Kaiserslautern, the scorer of two of the Watford UEFA goals was Ian Richardson. Carr and Banks would later pursue Richardson, but ultimately in vain when the player was at Chester, during the Cobblers' championship season.

It was the following term that Carlsberg night-shift worker Conroy spotted the cry for help from the Cobblers board in the *Chronicle & Echo* and mentioned it to his friend, knowing business was going well for Banks. 'How would you like to buy a football club?' he asked.

'Sure, why not?' was Banks' reply, his nonchalance somewhat taking his companion aback.

Contact was made, although the initial approach was not encouraging. Perhaps in a cynical age and in a town such as Northampton, which has never sought to place itself at the head of the queue, you can understand how no one was at the club to meet the pair, their phone call having been treated it seemed as an elaborate hoax.

'I was just told to hang around until someone turned up,' recalled Banks. Eventually, the opportunity to discuss the buy-out with secretary-cum-general manager Dave Bowen and Nev Ronson was arranged. Progress made, boxes ticked, the club had a new owner, the then second youngest chairman in the Football League, behind Derby's Ian Maxwell.

Like Banks, when he parted company with the club, Ronson never felt the urge to return, although the one exception to this was the Dave Bowen Memorial match against Arsenal in August 1996. The Cobblers defeated Arsenal 3-1 on that night in a fitting repeat score-line of the famous 1958 third round FA Cup which eventually led to a 1-3 defeat at Liverpool in the next round. To this day, Ronson claims he would have liked the privilege of being club President for more than the one day it actually materialised.

Banks needed, and was given, the support of his father Len in his new venture and it was something he cherished right up to the time of the latter's passing away in 1991. 'Dad was always at the games with me, along with my accountant Barry Blundell. If he didn't approve, I didn't do it. He was probably a keener supporter than I was. When I had to stand aside later on after losing a lot of money when the BCCI bank collapsed in the late 1980s, he was vociferous in his outcry against it.

'The whole business all started out quite innocently – a case of "let's have a look at it and see". You don't know what you are getting into, but it was an opportunity and it looked good on my CV! The football period was a nice time in my life and the type of hardship the directors all experienced with the ground and getting the fire certificate after the Bradford Fire Disaster probably helped.'

The immediate aftermath of the Bradford fire had serious implications for the County Ground, which had always been among the country's poor relations among stadia, with more than a touch of the eccentric thrown in. All of the main stand seats were instantly closed off, and it wasn't long before the top half was literally sliced off, leaving only the office and dressing rooms below, and the standing paddock, now exposed, in front. It wasn't until the Rochdale game on 1 March 1986 that the 400-seater Meccano Stand was opened.

It all presented an unexpected early brickbat in the path of Banks and his new board, and he admitted: 'If we had known what we were all letting ourselves in for, we probably wouldn't have done it. However, I still get a good sensation when I look back on it now and watch the old Gary Mabee video productions with all the highlights: the sensational 4-4 draw at Southend in the FA Cup, Richard Hill's tremendous goal against Tranmere and "Benji" getting the winner at Peterborough after performing that nutmeg on Wakeley Gage.'

Banks added: 'We were all pulling together. Everybody was working to the same end and it was all hands to the pump. I looked back on it afterwards and realised I was lucky – in many ways I got the best part of the bargain. Other people had the rubbish end. My business was solvent and I was able to buy the club for the same sort of money that you would pay for a three-bedroom house.

'We were coming to the end of an era in football because a lot of things were changing at around that time. There were the local Northampton business guys who formed the consortium who came on board and who did a lot of the work when the main stand was condemned after Bradford. They took a lot of the brunt of it.

'In the end we worked out that if the team was winning it really didn't matter too much about the ground, as long as it had a certificate to allow us to play at the County Ground, so we concentrated on the team. All those holes in the old Hotel End roof, I've heard all the old jokes about where Colin Cowdrey hit his sixes during the cricket season.'

Even when Banks did ultimately sell the club to Dick Underwood, it wasn't the end of the association, as he almost became involved again with the club years later in the aftermath of the near calamitous Michael McRitchie chairman era, when the club entered administration.

So much so, that you can almost see Banks' predecessor Ronson nodding in wise agreement. After all, he had spent eighteen years on the board from 1967 and had similarly worked with some 'good men' whose willingness to combine energies and work for free had fuelled an ambition of a new council-approved stadium while keeping the club afloat on ridiculously low budgets. 'When they walked away they never asked for their money back,' said Ronson.

Ronson's father Jack had moved to the town from Lancaster to work for the railways in Far Cotton and helped form Queen Eleanor FC in the

Northampton Town League. He remained loyal to his son to the end, even working late in life for the club's lottery drive as a collector alongside Roly Mills and organiser Geoff Moody.

Ronson himself graduated from the park scene to spend four years at First Division Luton Town as a hopeful centre-forward from 1949-53, endeavouring in vain to break through at a successful club who boasted such legends of the day as centre-half Syd Owen, Bernard Streten and Gordon Turner. 'I never really believed it would happen for me at Division One level, but it was good to be there at that time,' said Ronson.

Turning reflections back to the Cobblers he added: 'When we appointed Graham Carr he was on £13,000 p.a. and the budget for the whole club was only £120,000 – that included everything.'

Both well-intentioned bodies of men were to be disappointed with their stadium quests, Ronson on the Danes Camp, Mereway development by the old Towcester road in 1981, and Banks at Brackmills, now a thriving industrial estate on the Northampton ring road, close to the M1.

Summing up the efforts of his boardroom team in keeping the club afloat, Ronson reflected: 'There were a lot of good men who gave their time for nothing but, although one or two left the area at the same time, I think there was a feeling of disillusionment after we were knocked back on the stadium.'

People might have a rosy view of life as a football club director but Ronson remarked: 'I think one Friday night at Hartlepool summed it all up for me. Due to business I was late for meeting the team coach, which left without me. I drove all the way up to Hartlepool and back in the pouring rain and we lost the match 0-3. On top of that I suffered a puncture on the M1 coming home.' That was season 1968-69, the year the Cobblers dropped back to Division Four. Hartlepool went down with them and though he didn't know it at the time, Ronson had even more traumas still ahead of him.

Ronson's team of directors had been: Les Jaffa, Max Griggs, Trevor Hadland, Bob Brett, Geoff Adkins, Stuart Wilson and Eric Northover, while the club's consultant architect Derek Cox was also a considerable supporter.

Hadland was the son-in-law of Wally Penn, the club's chairman in the 1960s, while Griggs of course went on to found a dynasty at neighbours Rushden & Diamonds. At Northampton he became disillusioned with some of the treatment handed out to directors by supporters. The board took more than their fair share of flak from the terraces during the dark days and eventually it ground them down. A meek and mild individual, Griggs watched the Cobblers from the terraces for some time afterwards and it is always worth remembering he had not amassed his fortune through the Dr Marten boot industry during the time he spent at Northampton.

Banks had the local consortium backing, which comprised men such as Charlie Barham, Mark Deane, Barry Stonhill, Martin Pell, Dick Underwood, Grahame Wilson, Barry Hancock, Martin Church and Bob Church and (unrelated), who all came onto the board eventually.

Stuart Wilson and Northover, a harkback to the 1960s, remained for a short time, while Banks opened the eyes to the corridors of power to his old pal Conroy by giving him a seat on the board. A far cry, this, from time spent grafting at Carlsberg in the conditioning department. Conroy died prematurely at the age of 52 but his old pal was able to reflect on the excitement he had helped to generate.

'I think that meant more to him than any money,' said Banks.

At different times both Ronson and Banks believed their stadium projects were close to being approved by the Northampton developers. Ronson's £9 million, 25,000-seated stadium linked to a sports hall was part of a grander £30 million development which he believed would have brought employment and lasting benefits to the town. Its failure to materialise was a pattern which had precedents then, before being repeated since. Thirty years on, Ronson has still been known to gaze from a distance at where the lights would have shone from one of the town's highest peaks on Danes Camp to the south of the town by the old Towcester Road.

Perhaps, you reflect, the shimmering haze would have been detrimental to the landscape, but it would have been nice to find out.

For many years Ronson saved press articles highlighting the project, one a pithy account written by the *Chronicle & Echo* feature writer Chris Hilsden. The meat and drink style heading: 'Cobblers' victory after a great team performance' in no way does justice to a humorous piece which optimistically reflected on a council meeting whose members appeared to have the stadium already half-built in their minds. The sub-heading: Cobblers 34 Meanies 0 suggested one-way traffic, encouraged during an opening salvo which began with what old-school football hacks would describe as running copy:

'Right from the kick-off big Bruce Bunker created space on the left and turned the Meanies' full-back inside out before sending over a long centre. And there was wily midfielder David Walmsley, known as Artful Owl, bursting through from the right to steer the ball firmly with his head to put the Cobblers in the lead. And if anyone thought it could possibly have been an own-goal they were far too polite to say so.'

History confirms that an unscripted second leg brought something of a transformation and re-think. Perhaps as a football lover, whose clubs were Northampton and Luton, Ronson saw this one coming. For famous in Cobblers' folklore is the Boxing Day meeting of 1927 between these clubs when Northampton recovered from 1-5 down at half-time to win 6-5.

The project engineered by Banks' board saw plans for a £12 million project submitted to the local authority, funded by retail development with the club then leasing the stadium back. Given the urgency to remove the umbilical cord which united the town's football and cricket clubs, preventing advancement of both, and the built-in agreement to provide extra sporting facilities, it had plenty of plus points, which is probably one of the reasons Sixfields was finally born in 1994.

Estate agent Barry Stonhill was the man who persistently carried out negotiations with the local council for many years and it is a partial coincidence (although the extreme severity of the Cobblers' plight was undoubtedly a factor) that the Northampton consortium appeared on the scene at around the same time as Banks.

That was born from Stonhill's habit of playing a fortnightly game of snooker on a lunch time with Cheltenham & Gloucester Building Society manager Barham at the Conservative Club on the town's Billing Road. Stonhill, destined to later be the club chairman said: 'I had never been a particular supporter of the club, although my wife Jacqui was and had worked for them when they reached Division One in the 1960s. It wasn't that I wasn't interested, simply because I was still playing football at that time for Chesham in the Athenian League, and then later on for the ON Chenecks in Northampton.

'Charlie and I started talking when we got together, saying how bad it was that a town of Northampton's size was always applying for re-election. We wanted to do something to help. We approached Nev Ronson when the club was put up for sale but he was quite dismissive in a nice sort of way, saying he was talking to someone about selling the club – which turned out to be Derek Banks. When Banks bought the club we approached him and, although we were initially turned down, he quickly came back to us and accepted our offer of support. We would generate local business support in return for two seats on the board, which to begin with were taken up by Charlie and Mark Deane. We were known as "The Friends of the Cobblers".

'What turned out initially as a bit of a laugh suddenly became quite serious. I remember Mark and Charlie ringing me up after their first away match as directors at Burnley. They had been sitting in the Bob Lord stand in leather seats in the directors' box. After that a few people came out of the woodwork and joined up. In fact it was a bit "mob-handed",' but at least we pulled people together.'

Barham was a key integrator during the early stages when he filled a variety of roles, including 'spare-time' secretary when Bowen stood down from this role in 1986, but he died of cancer on the day the Cobblers played at Ipswich in the Littlewoods Cup the following year.

The Watford connection reverberates still further on closer inspection of Carr's management team, which was made up by coach Clive Walker, who has completed 50 years in football (fifteen at Northampton) from his time as a young Leicester City apprentice, and physiotherapist Denis Casey, who filled that capacity at both the County Ground and Sixfields for 23 years.

While Casey cannot be tied even to the most minute Watford thread, Frank Grande's statistical reference book *The Definitive Northampton Town FC* pinpoints Walker's place of birth as Watford, although the one-time Leicester, Cobblers and Mansfield defender defines it more precisely as Bushey. Perhaps that's just as well, for given our Watford-west coast obsession, we might otherwise have simply branded him as a railway coach.

Walker was born just months after the end of the war, and though a year younger than Carr, misses his birthday by just a day. He explained: 'My mother and father were both in the Navy but I moved to Leicester when I was just a baby.'

Tenuous Watford link then, but if ever a management team appeared moulded to work together, surely it was Carr, Walker and Casey. Carr and Walker had England youth and schoolboy honours, while like Carr, Walker made Division One appearances which would allow him to dine out on such stories, if he so chose.

Indeed, he played in the second leg of Leicester's 1965 League Cup final defeat by Chelsea. The Foxes were the holders of the competition, having beaten Stoke over two legs the year before. In the run to the 1965 final they memorably crushed local rivals Coventry 8-1 in the quarter-final at Highfield Road before winning both semi-final legs against Plymouth.

Leicester only trailed narrowly after losing the final's first leg 2-3 at Stamford Bridge, but the return was a goalless stalemate at Filbert Street. However, if anyone ever tells you accusingly that it was Northampton's long-time servant Clive Walker who missed a penalty in a League Cup final, they are (appropriately enough) wide of the mark. The Clive Walker they are alluding to was the former Chelsea and Sunderland player who missed a spot-kick at Wembley in 1985 when Sunderland were defeated 0-1 by Norwich.

The Leicester and Northampton Walker said: 'I had been playing regularly in the reserves at left-back but I played most of my first-team games there at right-back. I made my debut against Aston Villa in Division One but was moved to right-back after that. Mind you, that was almost the only time I did play in that position – most of my career was at left-back – it certainly was at Northampton.'

Chelsea became the first London side to win the League Cup and had a wealth of talent in their ranks, first-leg goalscorers Bobby Tambling, Terry Venables and Eddie McCreadie notable among them.

Walker recalled: 'I played 20 or so games for Leicester under Matt Gillies in Division One, including one against Manchester United at Old Trafford with George Best in the team, although he was switched inside that day and I found myself directly up against John Aston. We lost 0-1, with John Sjoberg unfortunate enough to get an own-goal. I also played against Aston Villa and West Ham a few times, as well as Birmingham City and Tottenham.'

The Walker-Carr connection was first forged in the Cobblers defence in Division Two in 1996-67 after Walker made the short move from Leicester. He explained: 'I probably should have stayed at Leicester but I was a young lad who wanted regular games. I remember it being very hard during that first season in the second division.'

The pair could hardly fail to get to know one another as they both lived in club houses in Barley Lane in Kingsthorpe and were directly over the road from one another. Even in those days, Carr was ever the practical prankster and recalled: 'I used to do things like put a note out for their milkman asking for extra cream and saying it was their daughter's birthday!'

Walker made 80 appearances for the Cobblers, scoring just one goal, in a 4-1 win at the County Ground against Orient in his first game back following a cartilage operation in December 1968. He moved to Mansfield Town in 1969, where he enjoyed six successful years for a variety of managers, namely Tommy Eggleston, Jock Basford, Danny Williams and Dave Smith. Williams was the man who took Swindon to their memorable 3-1 League Cup triumph over Arsenal in 1968-69 during two spells in charge at the Football League's other County Ground. Walker's undoubted highlight of his time at Field Mill included a notable run to the fifth round of the FA Cup in 1969-70 when the Stags were beaten 0-2 by Leeds at Elland Road after ousting Bury, Shrewsbury, Barnsley and Blackpool en route. That was the year Leeds marched on to play Chelsea in the final, losing 1-2 in a replay at Old Trafford after drawing 2-2 at Wembley.

Walker next met up with Carr during his non-league days at Chelmsford (he also played at Gravesend) while Carr was with Weymouth, but a much earlier return to Northampton meant he was already a familiar figure on the scene, long before Carr re-emerged.

Walker worked initially as a coach under Johnny Petts, which gave him a brief spell of caretaker charge before Mike Keen was appointed. Then, after Keen departed in March 1979, Walker had his first spell in charge before working once more as a coach when Bill Dodgin returned for a second spell of taking over the reins.

Always happier on the coaching ground, Walker's perseverance and loyalty at Northampton is to be applauded under the constant cash restrictions. After his second spell of management (February 1982 to May 1984) he happily stepped aside. The decision was taken before a 0-6 hammering at Peterborough at the end of April 1984 but even so, Walker, whose language could be colourful at the best of times, abandoned his favourite phrase 'frightening' in favour of something which more accurately reflected the mood, on a black night for the club.

Yet even here there was a sting in the tail. Walker walked away to help set up a YTS scheme at the club, an exacting enough task in itself, given the lack of resources within the club. When new man Tony Barton suffered his pre-season heart attack, it must have seemed that someone, somewhere up on high was having just a small amount of fun at his expense, even if the circumstances surrounding the hasty return to caretaker role were clearly no laughing matter.

There was simply no escaping the poisoned chalice that was the hot seat at Northampton Town FC. During those troubled times, it also briefly became a Leicester City old-boys team at the helm, as Walker found himself working alongside Richie Norman, who had filled the other full-back position during that 1965 League Cup final and who played in four Cup finals for the Foxes.

Norman had already been at the club as physiotherapist for a year, and later went on to occupy a similar role with Northamptonshire's cricketers, just across the boundary ropes.

After leaving the Cobblers in 1990, Walker teamed up with Carr again at Maidstone, Kettering, and Dagenham & Redbridge before moving to Kent in the late 1990s. Two spells in charge at Dover and summers working in the USA have kept alive his appetite for the game, and his most recent post has been as coach at Faversham Town, while also helping out with the Kent FA.

One of the supreme ironies and contested loyalties almost occurred during Walker and Carr's time at Kettering. They failed by just three points to win the GM Vauxhall Conference behind Kidderminster Harriers in 1994, with a side which included ex-Cobblers Warren Donald and Graham Reed as important cogs. This was the year the Cobblers finished bottom of the Football League, but they were saved relegation as the Harriers' Aggborough ground was not deemed suitable. Had the Poppies been crowned champions, Carr and Walker would have ousted their old club, as Rockingham Road had no such limitations.

Like chairman Banks, Carr was at one stage touted for a Northampton Town return. In 1993 It was widely believed he would come back after being approached by members of the Cobblers board and leave Rockingham Road.

I have particularly vivid memories of the night when Carr elected to stay put, which produced a 3-3 draw with Runcorn. My future wife Caroline was one of several extra local press who boosted the gate that night as she represented BBC Radio Northampton.

Football, it must be said, is not one of Caroline's preferred areas, yet as she was the only person present who possessed a microphone for the post-match analysis, she was pushed to the front of the queue by the otherwise male-dominated ruck to ask the key questions; a task she performed to her usual levels of high professionalism, despite the fact she would probably have rather been in a thousand other places that night.

It would be too glib and a little unkind to say the Cobblers' progress was merely pedestrian under Walker, but found extra gears under Carr. It was the mix of everything: coaching, tactical nous, team spirit and networking which reaped the rewards.

The combination of Walker's coaching and Carr's contacts prowess and motivational skills were clearly a subtle mix, and one which was recognised by Casey who had himself been a Cobblers youth player in the early 1960s and who turned his back on a career in engineering so he could work full time in football.

While his playing career fell short of the professional stage, he was a member of the first post-war United Counties League side to reach the first round of the FA Cup when Wellingborough Town were beaten 2-1 at Aldershot in 1965-66, nippy inside-forward Casey scoring the only goal of the game when Harwich & Parkeston were beaten 1-0 at the Dog & Duck in the fourth qualifying round.

Casey became an unsung but crucial third part of the management team after qualifying as a physiotherapist and initially helping out Carr at Nuneaton on odd occasions on match days when required. He said: 'I remember working with Graham in an FA Cup-tie at Wisbech where we won 6-0 and thinking the boot was on the other foot for me now as the giant rather than the giant killer, after my time at Wellingborough.

On Walker he offered: 'Coaching was definitely Clive's favourite area of the game. He was an excellent coach and well respected by the players. He had the ideal temperament for a coach. He could be forceful with the players if Graham felt they needed a rollicking but he would come along afterwards and pick them up again and get them going.'

Considering the relatively short 'route one' hop down the motorway, it should not be considered surprising that so many Watford-Northampton links exist, yet perhaps the coincidence is that so many have been prolific goalscorers, even before Hill's 1986-87 heroics.

The obvious starting point goes back to Cliff Holton's 54 goals for the club in 68 appearances between September 1961 and December 1962. Bobby Brown, who joined the Cobblers from The Hornets in 1963, topped the club's goalscoring charts during their only season in Division One, while Charlie Livesey followed Brown up the M1 in 1964 and netted in a Division One defeat at Burnley, having been a cult figure at Vicarage Road where he scored 26 times between 1962-64.

Since then, the aforementioned Reilly, John Fairbrother, Alan Mayes, Garry Thompson, Colin West and Allan Smart have been among goalgrabbers to have played for both clubs, while although he plied his trade as a midfield man, this section would not be complete without another reference to our network link man Ray Train, scorer of that memorable first goal against Mansfield on the night Banks was introduced to the Northampton crowd and who also spent time in a Hornets shirt.

My abiding memory of Train centres round a first round FA Cup-tie with VS Rugby in November 1984 in which he helped the Cobblers survive an embarrassing early exit by equalising in the final minute to make it 2-2. The Cobblers won the replay 1-0 at Butlin Road with a Wakeley Gage goal. Inevitably, the *Sports Pink* headline on the Saturday night read: 'Late Train on the Whistle.' If there has been a cuter or more fitting appraisal, I have yet to see it in print.

Not that the Watford-Northampton overlaps are exclusive to goalscorers: goalkeepers Steve Sherwood and Kevin Hitchcock; defenders Bryn Jones, Bill Baxter, Steve Terry, Tony Geidmintis, Sean Dyche, Des Lyttle, Gerard Lavin, Jason Drysdale, Charlie Bishop; and midfielders Paul Saunders, Peter Coffill, Richard Johnson and Neil Doherty have seen to that over the years. In fact, Baxter, who played over 400 times for Ipswich, is one of those rarities who notched up a Watford, Cobblers and Nuneaton treble. He went on loan to the Hornets before spending one season as player-manager with the Cobblers in 1972-73, before a brief spell at Nuneaton.

The Cobblers were only seventh favourites to win Division Four in 1986-87, the bookmakers rating them a 14-1 chance in the market behind such notable co-favourites as relegated Cardiff, and Lincoln and Leyton Orient who had finished the previous campaign in fifth place, albeit seven points behind promoted Port Vale. Also ahead of them in the market were Burnley and Wolves (10-1) and Colchester (11-1).

Yet for Walker and Casey, the back-up crew, who had witnessed a young side predominantly pulled together out of non-league, there was a strong feeling in the subconscious that 1986-87 would be special.

Casey said: 'You could see the players were learning from going full time and improving all the time. That second season at Northampton was the best job in the world. We had quality all over the pitch and it was as though we had 11 round pegs in 11 round holes and it is not very often you get that in football or life.'

Walker added: 'It was quite frightening really and a great team to be involved with. You always had the impression we were about to score. It didn't seem to matter if we went a goal down. You always had the feeling we were capable of then getting two or three.'

The players weren't the only people at the club working hard. The newly formed board were pulling together and boss Carr was permanently fired up, inspired by the task in hand. He recalled: 'I used to sometimes get a rollicking from my wife Christine for dropping the kids off so early at school in the morning. I think they used to be the first ones there at Weston Favell, as I was so anxious to get to work.'

The County Ground was a strange place from which to derive inspiration. There wasn't even a car park for the players, and when matches were being played during the cricket season, if they trained a mile away at the Old Northamptonians Sports Ground, players would often have to walk back through streets congested by Northants CCC supporters.

Another quirk was the clock. As a player in the 1960s, Carr recalled looking across the cricket square to the clock above the cricket pavilion, telling you how long there was left in a game. During 1986-87 Casey, Walker and Carr sat with their backs to the clock and didn't have to worry. They would regularly glance at one another while sitting in the dugout, imbued with a great feeling of optimism and expectation. One of them would say to the other: 'We must be due for a goal.'

Then, even if the Hotel End crowd weren't singing the familiar terrace chant at that precise moment, they could be fairly confident about one thing: 'We're going to score in a minute.' And invariably they did.

CHAPTER THREE

Flights of Fancy

I vividly remember gazing dreamily out of the window during the return flight home from Geneva to Gatwick, especially as it dipped for the first time beneath the clouds late on that September Saturday afternoon in 1986, bringing the green of the Sussex countryside into complete view. A quick check at my watch confirmed what I already knew to be true – as long as Graham 'Rambo' Reed had been up to his tricks that afternoon, the Cobblers should be about to enter injury-time at the Vetch Field in their sixth Division Four league match of the 1986-87 season.

While I had spent a pleasant week in Coppet in Switzerland catching up with an old pal from my banking days, there had still been the odd anxiety twinge at going 'absent with leave' so early in my new working brief of following the fortunes of Northampton Town FC for the *Chronicle & Echo*.

The eyebrows of sports editor Dave Jones, not a man normally given to shows of remonstration, had twitched and been raised mildly when I had first mentioned the subject of 'skipping' a few fixtures so early in the autumn. After all, I had only joined my home town evening newspaper in the May after two years on the weekly *Northants Post* and was still establishing my credentials.

Weeks of churning out the local park cricket and swimming reports had been interlaced with a personalised prediction slant on who would contest the World Cup final that summer in Mexico City. Sub-editor Dave Hickey, never one to sit on the fence and the man responsible for inserting the famous tongue-in-cheek 'telephone 31553' paragraph which had brought Derek Banks running, had not been able to display any of his quirks on this occasion. The headline simply screamed out 'Argentina and France' to my avid reader tucked away in the Northampton suburb of Bellinge – well, at least I managed to get it 50 per cent right!

Sadly, Hickey is no longer with us but in many respects I owe him a debt of thanks for my succession to Keith Hursthouse as the Cobblers football writer. It had been a childhood dream since the early days of primary school and a task I would carry out with varying degrees of efficiency for the next four seasons.

Early in the spring, I had bumped into Hickey in the Mailcoach (a popular watering hole of the time for Northampton hacks) and located conveniently just over the road from the Post Group's imaginatively named Newspaper House. He told me that *Chron* editor Phil Green was seeking a new football scribe for the 1986-87 campaign as Hursthouse, a man with a young family, was keen to move to a more straightforward subbing job on the desk, cutting out for him the humdrum travel to away matches to such delightful destinations as Hartlepool, Torquay and Swansea.

In fact, Hickey put it rather more succinctly. 'He's that desperate, you could walk into Phil's office and call him a "****" and he would still give you the job!' he smirked, before returning more seriously to his pint of Courage Director's bitter and the day's racing results from Fontwell Park. Perhaps this explains the muted celebrations when I was appointed a month or so later, although I can't recall being quite so brash during the interview. As I was also following in the footsteps of my father's cousin, Michael Beesley, who had covered the Cobblers' fortunes during their only Division One season of 1965-66 (see *A Season in the Sun*) a journey which began 21 years later in Division Four hardly suggested immediate fame and fortune. No mention of Manchester United, Liverpool or Arsenal here.

Confidence, though, is an important catalyst in bringing success and a feel-good mood certainly abounded, something which exuded warmly from the *Chronicle & Echo* offices on Upper Mounts in the summer of 1986. While they had dropped their role as shirt sponsors from the previous campaign, editor Green had the foresight to score a well-targeted publicity goal by issuing a challenge to the club: 'Win the league title and we'll give you £10,000!' the newspaper stands proudly proclaimed in the build-up. In fact the cost of the publicity was just £1,000 plus appropriate betting duty which stood in place in those days.

However, all things in life are relative, and Swansea, a distant, foreign outpost on a Saturday afternoon for football scribes, is definitely the place for me to start my season review, even though five unbeaten league matches preceded it.

Apart from my naturally perverse nature (of course, I wasn't actually at the match), the reason for this is quite simple. In a season which was quite unforgettable, the 21-match unbeaten league run which followed the 1-2 defeat at Swansea on that Saturday afternoon up to St Valentine's Day 1987 was absolutely awesome. Not just the icing on the season's cake, but the whole splendid range of Devon clotted cream and raspberry jam toppings (I much prefer raspberries to strawberries or any other fruit you care to mention).

Perversely, it probably helped establish my 'lucky talisman' tag for the season, although I'm not sure that explains my other embarrassing unscheduled absence that season, at Crewe on a Friday night. The Cobblers won 5-0, yet I was limping home somewhat crestfallen, after three hours stuck on the M1 due to the havoc caused by spillage from a petrol tanker. Thanks to a hurried phone call from colleague and deputy sports editor Brian Barron to Cheshire, the *Chron* still carried a report the next night although I lost a few brownie points, I felt a little unfairly.

Of those 21 memorable matches, seventeen were won, only four ending with the points shared. Hartlepool, Wrexham, Exeter and Tranmere played that minor party-pooping role. Of course, it wasn't just the fact these matches almost exclusively proved a cakewalk, it was the manner of the victories. In that period, 65 goals were scored and 24 conceded, which meant a rough average of 3-1 wins over that third of the season.

Remember the mind-boggling 6-3 Tuesday night win at Halifax? Not many people do, because the crowd was only 1,034. That's just 92 more people than the infamous 942 for the Chester match eighteen months earlier. Over the years it seems every Cobblers fan I have ever met insisted they were there to such an extent I suspect the actual crowd was more like 10,942. Perhaps it was simply they all had sore throats and the place was very eerie.

No, I really was there for Chester and Halifax, although I didn't register on the official count, as press get in for free. The Halifax night triggered a Cobblers mini-burst of 26 goals in seven league games with a match aggregate of 40 (averaging almost seven a game). You tend to get blasé about it: Halifax 6-3, Aldershot 4-2, Cambridge 3-2, Burnley 4-2, Hereford 3-2, Stockport 3-0 and Hartlepool 3-3. No wonder I then fell into the spoilt-child trap when we went down to Brisbane Road on a Tuesday night and only won 1-0 at Leyton Orient. You can imagine Carr's reaction when I began the press conference with the immortal words: 'Well that wasn't very good, was it!' or words to that effect.

If I started to learn a lesson for life during those goal-happy days it was to fully appreciate your good moments. As you must be well aware, there are plenty which don't even tick half the boxes. Staring down at those green fields around Gatwick on that Saturday afternoon definitely meant a good day for me, even if it wasn't for Carr's men at the Vetch Field. It will surprise few to learn that when the Cobblers did lose again in the league that season, Swansea were the visitors.

Incidentally, there's one cameo tale of Swansea trips I can never help repeating, even though it doesn't relate to 1986-87. I might have escaped the thrilling drive past Port Talbot Steel Works on this occasion, but the equilibrium of life has a habit of balancing out. A little over two years later (in mid-October to be precise) club photographer Pete Norton and

I endured a nightmare near five-hour car journey there, and I eventually hauled myself into the elevated press-box on stilts at 3.03pm to find the phone ringing and my frantic copy-taker Glenys Holden beside herself with anxiety on my account.

A forgettable afternoon, which saw the Cobblers lose 0-1, had at least attained a degree of serenity as we drove back along the M4 that evening, past the aforementioned Steel Works which seemed to spit fire like Welsh dragons in the darkness, satisfying ourselves with such trite remarks as: 'Well, at least we don't have to go back there again this season.'

It was in the good old days when they drew the first round of the FA Cup on Radio Two, and coincidentally, this was the night, after the fourth qualifying round had been played that day. Of course, you can guess what's coming up next. Pottering along at a steady 65mph, a sense of wheel-control and humour almost went completely out of the window when out popped No 57 (Swansea City) versus No 36 (Northampton Town). I can't pretend to exactly remember the numbers, but I'm sure you get the general picture. Season ticket at the Vetch anyone?

It rather put a dampener on our ritual Saturday night of tuning into Keith Fordyce and *Beat the Record*, once our post-match summaries were done (simple pleasures!). We didn't even find it as funny as usual when we heard the inevitable caller (who always seemed to be from Norway) who hadn't a clue about the answer to the musical poser, but simply wanted to hear himself on air. Some 35 days later we went back to Swansea and the Cobblers lost 1-3, although on this occasion we avoided traffic jams and congestion on the Severn Bridge and its approaches.

The championship season had begun in alarming fashion at Scunthorpe, the first game I ever covered for the *Chronicle & Echo*. In many ways just 90 minutes of football would encapsulate the next four years: 2-0 up after ten minutes, drew 2-2! Looking back, it seemed to neatly sum up my four-season experience of directly reporting yo-yo club Northampton Town.

However, if ever you want convincing nothing in life is predictable, the summer build-up proved that. Less than a month before the big kick-off, I interviewed the former Manchester City, Middlesbrough, Cardiff and Portsmouth striker Paul Sugrue, who had scored twice during the 1985-86 run in during what would be a brief stop at the County Ground.

With Trevor Morley injured in pre-season, it appeared a 'God given' certainty Sugrue would start the season in a Cobblers' shirt, and the confident piece in the *Chron* cried out: 'Just watch us go, beams confident Sugrue.' While the prediction surrounding the Cobblers' fortunes proved accurate enough, it omitted to say that Sugrue, who ironically later had a short spell as manager of Nuneaton, would play no part in the glory, quitting the club before the season started. Perhaps the headline should actually have read: 'Just watch me go,' then everyone would have understood the full meaning.

Carr later confessed he hadn't been surprised to see the nomadic striker walk away. Perversely, the reverse side of the coin was that tough-as-teak Morley, against all expectations, lined up at The Old Show Ground on 23 August.

It seems the demands of Carr and Walker's ultra-fit regime took its toll on Sugrue, as he said in the article: 'I knew Graham Carr and trained with Northampton last August, then had to go back to Portsmouth for a rest. It is so much harder training here and I realised how unfit I was when I came back in March.'

To be fair to Sugrue, the training schedule was alarming. Graham Reed recalled: 'We would lose all those evening friendlies on the northeast to people such as Blue Star and Blyth Spartans, but no one realised we had been running and training on the beach at 7am.'

So it was Morley in and Sugrue nowhere at Scunthorpe, an occasion full of memorable stats in the Cobblers' last appearance at the Old Show Ground on 23 August 1986 (The Iron moved to Glanford Park in 1988). It was the start of what was billed in football 'the season of change', with Division One being reduced to 21 clubs (twenty by 1988-89) while promotion/relegation play-offs were brought in for the first time, and the club ending bottom of Division Four being automatically relegated for the first time.

The Cobblers and Scunthorpe entered the spirit of the occasion with seven players making debuts, including Bobby Coy, Eddie McGoldrick and Dave Gilbert for the Cobblers (Ron Green, Alan Birch, Steve Johnson and Dave McLean for the Iron), and the season portents were immediately sunnier than the August sunshine for travelling supporters. Just as twelve months earlier, the Cobblers had travelled north to face opponents decked out in claret and light blue and scored two goals, this time in reverse order. However, the important point this time was exactly that. They earned a point.

Hill fired the Cobblers ahead after five minutes, firing in from eight yards as a result of Chard's long throw, while Reed struck the second, reacting sharply from Gilbert's corner. It was this strike to make it 2-0 which set the bells ringing for the statistics men. The last time a Cobblers full-back had scored on the opening day of the season, Barry Tucker's speculative 50-yarder (perhaps a hopeful punt?) at Huddersfield in 1975-76, the club had gone on to win promotion under Bill Dodgin. Fact!

Better still, the last time the Cobblers had drawn 2-2 on the opening day of the season (against Bristol Rovers) they had gone on to win a title (Division Three in 1962-63) for only the second time in their history. Fact! Curiously, they won 2-1 at Scunthorpe on the opening day in Division Two in 1963-64, yet finished only eleventh.

The only other precedent for winning titles was the Southern League in 1908-09, when the club scored an opening-day 2-0 win at New Brompton, which is now Gillingham. Was it a coincidence the Cobblers then played at Gillingham on the Monday night in the Littlewoods Cup? I rather think not. Someone up on high was clearly organising all this.

Whatever the supernatural effect, you can see how much these moments must be treasured. Curiously, on the three occasions the Cobblers have won league titles in their history, they finished in that semi-threatening position of eighth the season before. Fact!

For Rambo Reed, the remarkable Scunthorpe statistic was the fact that only two Cobblers goals he would net in 131 appearances for the club arrived on the opening day of consecutive seasons, playing firstly as a centre-forward and then as a right-back.

Reed actually had the chance to join Scunthorpe when he joined Barnsley from school on the same day as a certain David Speedie, as well as future Leicester midfielder Ian Banks, but opted to start his career at the Oakwell Ground instead.

Reed said: 'I was at the same school, Adwick Park in Doncaster, as David Speedie, although he was a year above me. I was a Leeds supporter as a lad, so imagine what it was like to make my Barnsley debut at home to Worksop in the first round of the FA Cup, alongside the player-manager at the time, Allan Clarke, who was a Leeds legend to all and certainly to me.'

The reality of working close at hand with Clarke soon destroyed any idolatry for Reed, who earned his debut chance after former Coventry and Sheffield Wednesday striker Brian Joicey was injured in a match at York, which was later diagnosed as a minor stroke.

Reed scored two goals in the 5-1 win over Worksop and recalls: 'I went on a night out to Sheffield dog track that evening, where I was having a meal with some friends. I bought the local *Green 'Un* and found I was on the front and back pages, so I bought another five copies.

After two years as an apprentice and one as a professional and making just a handful of appearances, Reed dropped out of the League and signed for Frickley, while Speedie went to Darlington in 1980, without ever hitting the target as a Barnsley player. Matters would change somewhat when John Neal signed him for Chelsea for £80,000 in 1982.

Years later Speedie turned up at a midweek Cobblers match in London and persuaded Reed's boss Carr to allow his old team-mate to train at Chelsea for a couple of days at a time when he was partnering Kerry Dixon in attack for the Londoners. Reed was amazed Carr allowed this to happen and said: 'I'm sure if I had asked the gaffer whether I could train at Chelsea for two days he would have said "no"!'

Living in the Woodlands area of Doncaster, Reed's father and uncle worked in the pit at Brodsworth Colliery and eventually he was able to get a job shovelling coal while combining that with playing football for Frickley Athletic. As a striking miner, at least in the football sense, Reed established himself at the club and was top scorer for the side with 22 goals, as well as earning the Player of the Year vote in 1984-85, the season before he joined the Cobblers.

Not surprisingly he recalled: 'There was a big coal fire in the dressing room at Frickley and the whole place could be quite fierce. I remember one match with Stalybridge Celtic during the miners' strike in 1985 when the match was stopped four or five times and finished at about 5.30pm. There were supporters throwing great lumps of brick at one another – we won 1-0 and I scored the winner with a screaming free-kick.'

Coming from this sort of background, few people who saw Reed play could be surprised he cultivated a 'hard man' image. He had always wanted to play as an attacker, in fact he started as a youngster on the right wing. Yet Carr clearly had him in mind primarily for rugged defensive duties. 'He could always win a battle and kick the ball a long way,' he said.

Carr recalled watching Reed in Frickley's 3-1 FA Trophy quarter-final defeat at Wealdstone in 1985 and said: 'I knew the Frickley chairman Mike Twiby quite well and I was impressed by what I learned – the wholehearted way Graham played his football, considering he often arranged his shifts down the pit with matches. He would come straight off the back of a shift and play with total commitment before sleeping in the coach all the way home. At Wealdstone he was up against one of the Cordice brothers, Neil and Alan – in fact Alan had a spell at Northampton in the late 1970s, and they were tough opponents.'

Versatility counts for much, and during his four seasons at the club Reed wore eight different shirt numbers (odd numbers were presumably a problem as he omitted 1, 3, 7 and 11).

'I still wanted to play up front but after my debut at Burnley in 1985-86 the gaffer switched me to right-back, although I still insisted on wearing the No 9 shirt for a while,' (fifteen times that season).

If the Cobblers' hard-earned point at Scunthorpe was a game of two halves (some pundits cruelly suggested Mark Schiavi turned the game at

2-0 by replacing groin injury victim Hill early in the second half), this was also a day when another Division Four venue provided four halves. The answer to this quaint trivia poser is Hartlepool's Victoria Ground, where Pool drew 1-1 with Cardiff City in the afternoon before a Division Three contest was drawn 2-2 in the evening between Middlesbrough and Port Vale. Middlesbrough's Ayresome Park ground was in the hands of the Official Receiver until 2 September and couldn't be used.

Football history was made at Gillingham on the Monday night, with Gills' boss Keith Peacock being the first to use two substitutes in the form of Mel Eves and Paul Collins in the 1-0 Littlewoods Cup first leg win over the Cobblers. This was the first time two had been allowed, and this tie was played in advance of all the others that week.

The Gills had opened their Division Three campaign on the Saturday with a 2-1 win at Newport and were destined to lose in the play-off final that season to Swindon, with Harry Redknapp's Bournemouth winning the section by three points from Bruce Rioch's Middlesbrough, who had started the season in a virtual state of bankruptcy.

In fact, the Kent club were responsible for dragging Boro's north-east rivals Sunderland down into Division Three for the first time in their history in the play-off semi-finals, before ultimately losing 0-2 to Swindon after a third meeting between the clubs at Selhurst Park. This proved with hindsight what a tough hurdle it was for the Cobblers. Despite Donald's absence due to food poisoning, Aidy Mann stepping in, Hill was passed fit and played and Carr's men held out for 87 minutes. They actually did rather better than that, going closest to scoring on a night when the torrential rain poured down relentlessly. Two efforts by Morley within a minute either side of the half-hour came closest to breaking the deadlock.

Gleasure pulled off the save of the night after 72 minutes, when he kept out a low drive from Martin Robinson, but he was beaten late on when Mark Weatherley struck with a shot on the turn following a short corner.

Weatherley was a fitting name for a match-winner on a night of endless precipitation and, as usual, there was a somewhat offbeat tale to sum it all up. It involved club photographer Norton, who was asked by referee Darryl Reeves to remove his bright yellow mackintosh at the start of the second half as it was clashing with the Cobblers' away strip. Norton's reaction was understandably one of reluctance, horror and confusion in conditions more akin to the opening scenes of a scary Hitchcock movie than a trip to the Priestfield Stadium. His protests of: 'Wasn't it clashing in the first half?' and 'Why has it taken 48 minutes to work this one out?' held little water (if you'll forgive the pun) with match official Reeves.

Norton recalled: 'The night was like something out of a Biblical flood and I was sitting on a stool wearing a mackintosh which was more like a bivouac, as it more or less covered me down to my ankles. The funny thing was that none of the other photographers even bothered to go out that night as the conditions were so bad. I remember joining them in the two-tier press-box after the referee said his piece, as I was hardly likely to take off the mackintosh and sit there in my jumper with Noah about to starting building his Ark outside.'

The legacy of that night was that whenever Norton returned to Gillingham over the years to come, he was reminded of the occasion in the downpour by the Kent camera crew, which he was able to wear like a badge of honour.

He claims his only comparable claim to fame was at Southend on Boxing Day. Flanked by the division's leading scorer in Hill, en route to the players' bar, he was asked by an enthusiastic fan for his autograph. With Hill falling into fits of hysterics beside him, Norton was only too keen to offer advice: 'I think this is the guy you really want,' he said.

Before the League Cup home leg, the Cobblers hosted Torquay on the Sunday afternoon, after the rest of the division did battle on the Friday night and the Saturday afternoon. No one was making a remarkable start, with only Cambridge notching back-to-back victories, 2-1 at relegated Wolves and 1-0 at home to Halifax.

Donald returned to the line-up against the Gulls, who had drawn 1-1 with Burnley in their opener. However, as a side who were trying to avoid finishing bottom for the third year running, it wasn't expected to be the sternest test.

The first home match of 1986-87 was frankly a disappointment, not helped by a hard pitch and meeting a Torquay side who were intent on defence. After their ambitions were thwarted by Benjamin's mis-hit shot at the end of the first half, which bobbled embarrassingly over Jan Smeulders, Carr was disparaging of the opponents, saying: 'I would never let a side of mine go out and play like that. I would rather get beat 0-4 and entertain than defend like that. They didn't seem interested in going forward.'

The Torquay match may not have been memorable as a spectacle and it was certainly far too early for the Northampton public to cotton on fully as to what was about to unfold before them. Crowd figures at the County Ground stepped up progressively from this point.

However, the fact that Benjamin should prove to be the match winner in a 1-0 success, the first of three goals for the striker in as many tight consecutive games, was an indicator to one of the crucial plots of the season. While 'Benji' might not have been the Cobblers' top scorer in this season, he had been in the previous two, and his ability to consistently get on the scoresheet was to prove a major factor. Although he netted three hat-tricks and five doubles in his time with the Cobblers, the Benjamin haul of 23 goals in 1986-87 came in 23 different matches, even though he featured in all 55 league and cup games. Of those goals, fourteen arrived in contests where Town either won by the odd goal, or drew. The only match in which he scored that was lost was the 2-3 defeat at Fulham in the Freight Rover Trophy in January. That had to be completely different – he netted with a diving header!

This wasn't a bad record for a player whose Cobblers' career started with him not even able to make the starting line-up. He was sitting on the bench at kick-off during their 0-5 crushing loss at Exeter on the opening day of 1984-85. Even though he came on in the second half, it appears remarkable with hindsight he wasn't an automatic choice. Rarely can a player have made such a dramatic transformation to becoming such a vital cog.

From watching home games and carrying out a fair amount of interrogation on away matches in those early days, I quickly cottoned on to the fact that Benjamin was a rare jewel in a struggling outfit. The eleventh match of the Tony Barton season was a case in point, when he scored his first two Cobblers goals in a 3-0 win at Wrexham's Racecourse Ground, only the second victory of the campaign, before trumping that performance four days later with a hat-trick in a 4-0 romp against Aldershot.

That match proved to be a turning point for Benjamin, who up until this point had been a midfield player. After getting injured and missing matches with Port Vale and Scunthorpe, he came on as a substitute at Southend for the last twenty minutes in attack and continued in that role at Wrexham and indeed for the rest of his career.

The year before I joined the *Chronicle & Echo* I occasionally had to order match copy from away fixtures on a Tuesday night for the weekly *Northants Post*, which had a Wednesday morning copy deadline. On these days it was not unusual for me to visit the offices at around 10pm to take the phone call from our designated 'freelance' first hand. It was surreal enough in those days for the Cobblers to win any match, let alone 3-0 away from home.

However, on top of all that, the Wrexham reporter filing the copy went by the name of James Bond and I let my imagination run riot at the possibilities. 'Licence To Kill at The Racecourse?' I pondered. In Northampton that usually meant just the latest park mugging. On New Year's Day 1985 (again a Tuesday) I was again ordering freelance copy, this time from Stockport County. Benjamin was again on target on that occasion in a 2-4 defeat, but this time the author of the prose was none other than Howard Jones, not I believe the same one as the singer-songwriter who had hits around that time with *What Is Love?* and *Like To Get To Know You Well*. It came as a disappointment to learn that the latter release in 1984 was apparently designed to embody the spirit of the Los Angeles Olympic Games and not an oblique reference to the Cobblers' man-to-man marking system.

Such high-profile freelance football names left me wondering who else might be lurking on the freelance football circuit. By the time the *Post* issue of February 1985 came around, I was fully expecting to relay 'Halifax Town 1 Northampton Town 0, by Winston Churchill'. Perhaps the subsequent report could be entitled: 'Close shave at The Shay – but no cigar!' Certainly, like Churchill, the Cobblers knew all about the wilderness years, and didn't the manager bear a certain resemblance?

The fact that Benjamin took a while to blossom with the Cobblers is also reflected in his early career, although by the time he hung up his boots he had at various times been attached to twelve different league clubs, playing for all of them barring Notts County. Sheffield United, County, Peterborough, the Cobblers, Cambridge, Chester, Exeter, Southend, Luton, Brentford and Wigan. The list isn't endless, it simply appears to be.

The beginning of Benjamin's career was full of what seemed limitless potential from the moment he made his Sheffield United debut as a seventeen-year-old towards the end of the 1978-79 season. On Saturday, 21 April 1979 the Cobblers were nicking a useful Division Four point from a 2-2 draw at Halifax, but it was a momentous day for Benjamin two levels higher, coming on as a substitute for Sheffield United at Cardiff City's Ninian Park.

However, it was arguably more remarkable for ex-Cobbler John Buchanan, who had left the County Ground after four seasons in 1974, but being a sucker for punishment came back for two more in the early 1980s, after seven years with The Bluebirds.

Recalling those early years, Benjamin said: 'I had played for England Under-18s in a tournament in Yugoslavia 1979. I came on for the last 30 minutes against Germany, played against Poland and in other games. There were people such as Paul Walsh, Paul Allen, Terry Gibson, Colin Pates and Gary Mabbutt around me in that team.'

Benjamin's youthful experience had even seen him blooded for twenty minutes as a raw sixteen-year-old in a friendly against a River Plate side at Bramall Lane which featured six of the side who had helped home nation Argentina win the World Cup the summer before, beating Holland 3-1 in the final. Benjamin said: 'There were players such as the goalkeeper Ubaldo Fillol [who did not play in the World Cup finals] and the captain Daniel Passarella in the River Plate side. The match was arranged as part of the deal when Sheffield United signed Alex Sabella.'

Such a baptism bred expectation for Benjamin and he said: 'Harry Haslam was the manager of The Blades, but while I was expected to be the first of the young crop there to get into the side, I was actually the last. I remember expecting to make my debut in a match at Burnley but the boss took me out when it rained a lot that morning and the pitch turned heavy. I eventually got my chance in the match at Cardiff. I came on at 0-0 and we actually went on to lose the match 0-4, with John Buchanan getting a hat-trick. I remember playing in midfield with none other than Bruce Rioch alongside me.'

Cobblers fans who fondly remember the 1970 Hotel End terrace chant of 'Bu-Bu-Buchanan' will have some sympathy for Benjamin that afternoon. The Scottish midfield man made a name for himself scoring spectacular pot-shots. He certainly managed to put the cannon in Buchanan. That day brought his only league hat-trick at the end of one of two seasons in which he managed to top score for the Welsh club.

'He was banging them in from all angles,' recalled Benjamin, whose first full start for the Blades came in the final match of that season at home to Leicester, when the hosts needed to win 9-0 to stay up. Perhaps someone told Benjamin it was 90-0, as he scored a penalty in the first minute to set the ball rolling.

'John Matthews had just come back from injury and usually took the penalties but didn't fancy it, and someone piped up: "Benji takes them for the reserves", so I stepped forward and beat Mark Wallington,' the Cobblers striker recalled. That wasn't the end of the matter, as Benjamin also equalised in the last minute, putting away another spot-kick.

An auspicious start, even if the Blades were relegated with Millwall and Blackburn, Charlton staying up by a point. Benjamin recalls one of his last visits to his mum Elsie in Nottingham years later and discovering to his surprise, that she had kept a match report of the Leicester game.

However, his Sheffield career was a brief one and involved a missed penalty at the start of the following Division Three campaign in a drawn 1-1 League Cup-tie with Doncaster when Benjamin struck a post. However, before his £100,000 move to West Brom, he accepted the chance to set the record straight. 'I played in the next game with Swindon. I was directly up against Chris Kamara, who appeared huge to me, and went on to be the well-known Sky TV pundit. We were awarded a penalty which I scored and I remember our defender Tony Kenworthy telling me I had a lot of bottle. We won the game 2-1.'

The move to the Hawthorns followed just five matches in the Blades' line-up which prompted a call-up for Benjamin for England Under-18 training at Lilleshall but the odd 'out of hours' scrape during the Yugoslavia trip hadn't been forgotten and he wasn't picked again, even though he was described by John Cartwright, working with England boss Ron Greenwood at the time, as the most improved squad member. 'I was just a young lad in Yugoslavia and stayed out late one night,' Benji recalled. 'I didn't know what was right or wrong but I remember Ron Atkinson asking me why my behaviour letter from that tour wasn't a good one when I went to West Brom.'

Although the chance to switch to Atkinson and a Division One outfit appeared a dream opportunity, it didn't prove the happiest of times in the young player's career – and it prompted a three-year spell when his football was largely reserve-orientated. He recalled: 'The exact fee paid by West Brom was £138,000, which at the time was a record for a teenager, although Steve Mackenzie beat that just two weeks later when he went to Manchester City from Crystal Palace for £250,000.' Ironically, Mackenzie joined West Brom at a time just after Benjamin left the Hawthorns in 1981.

Benji added: 'Most of the first year there, I hated it, and Harry Haslam said if I wasn't enjoying it, I could come back to Sheffield. I went to see Ron Atkinson and told him that was what I wanted but he fobbed me off anyway, as he wanted me to stay. I think Sheffield needed the money. In Birmingham I was in a big city with a lot of the players living miles away. For three months I lived in a hotel with Peter Barnes and Gary Owen, but then I moved into a flat with my sister Lorinda for a year.'

Gradually, Benjamin's life in Birmingham improved and he struck up a rapport with the midfielder Remi Moses who eventually followed Atkinson to Old Trafford in 1981. While first-team opportunities were limited at The Hawthorns (he played only twice) Benjamin said: 'Big Ron used to take me away with the first team when Bryan Robson had been called up by England. In fact, I made my debut coming on at Ipswich in midfield when Tony Godden was injured and Bryan Robson went in goal. I made my full debut at the end of the season in a 0-0 draw at Leeds, alongside Robson and Moses.'

Moses' departure to Old Trafford prompted Benjamin's own departure, as his relationship with Atkinson's replacement Ronnie Allen was cool, to say the least. Matters came to a head on the day of Moses' departure, when the player asked Benjamin to give him a lift to the station.

'Ronnie Allen was there and told me that if I did that I was finished at West Brom so I told Remi to "get in",' said Benjamin.

Even from here, the path to the County Ground was not exactly direct, a brief link-up with his brother Tristan at Notts County before two years at Peterborough under Martin Wilkinson and then John Wile, managers with whom he had contrasting relationships. Wilkinson, an excellent coach with a fine eye for a player, later managed both Carlisle and the Cobblers.

Benjamin came to the Cobblers after falling out of favour with Wile, although his move bore an element of chance. He recalled: 'I had been released by Posh and bumped into my old team-mate Mario Ippolito in the town. He told me Clive Walker had contacted him about having a trial at Northampton and suggested I speak to them. I didn't do anything about it initially, but then I saw Mario again and we both went for trials there. As it turned out, Clive could only take one of us and it was myself who made the move.

'It was quite late in the summer and I remember sitting in Tony Barton's office with Phil Cavener when he told us he would like us both to join, but could only offer us £100 a week. I looked at Phil and we both thought we couldn't sign for that, and said so. Tony raised it to £120 and we accepted. It must be the only time two players have known what wage the other was on.' Ironically, Benjamin recalls then playing a pre-season friendly for the Cobblers at Carr's Nuneaton which was lost 1-3, leaving him to reflect: 'Well they don't look a bad side for non-league.'

Although Benjamin scored the bulk of his career goals for the Cobblers, Southend (1990-92) comes next on the list and he is still fondly remembered in Roots Hall folklore for scoring the only goal in a match at Bury towards the end of the 1990-91 season which earned promotion to Division One for the first time in their history. It can still be viewed on 'You Tube'. Benjamin executes a classic turn and low shot inside the penalty area at a time when his side are down to ten men, following the dismissal of Pat Scully, a former Arsenal central defender who had earlier spent time on loan at the Cobblers.

Pace was not Benji's forte – touch, control and vision undeniably were his strong points. Carr recalled that Benjamin's Exeter boss Terry Cooper had once described the 1986-87 Player of the Year as the only black man he knew who couldn't run, but Benjamin has his own slant on the tale, involving one of his favourite bosses David Webb, when at Southend.

'Webby told Terry Cooper I was the quickest player he had ever known, to which Cooper retorted: 'Benji's not quick! Webby replied that 'up there' [indicating his head] I was ten yards quicker than anyone.'

As a link-up player for the Cobblers, with Morley in attack, Benjamin proved a perfect foil. Between the pair, they were adept at holding the ball up and bringing others into play.

After netting the only goal against Torquay, Benjamin quickly followed up by netting on the Wednesday night at home to Gillingham before then scoring on the Saturday in the 2-1 success at Rochdale.

The Gillingham game ended in a 2-2 draw, and saw the Cobblers bow out of the Littlewoods Cup 2-3 on aggregate. The match was watched by Oxford boss Maurice Evans, whose Division One side thrashed the Gills 6-0 in the next leg of the next round before drawing 1-1 away. However, as the draw hadn't been made at this stage, he must have been gifted with second sight, useful when spying on future opposition.

Chief instigator of the Cobblers' downfall was Tony Cascarino, whose Republic of Ireland career had begun the year before in their World Cup qualifying campaign when he had played three times. Cascarino cancelled out Bobby Coy's fourteenth-minute opener and repeated the trick just three minutes after Benjamin had restored the Cobblers' advantage nine minutes from time.

Loan defender Coy was one of the unsung heroes of the Cobblers' campaign, yet he played a vital support role, especially early in the season when Russell Wilcox missed the first nine league games after sustaining an injury in a pre-season friendly at West Brom after a challenge with Steve Bull, who started to make his name on a grander scale just months later after moving to Black Country rivals Wolves.

Coy was Birmingham born and his career started at Molineux, yet he was capped at Under-15 England level as a goalkeeper. Defensive versatility was his game, as he operated competently as a full-back and in the centre of defence. He had twice played against the Cobblers for Chester in 1985-86. In fact, he missed only two matches, but despite being named player of the year in a promotion-winning side, had been released by Harry McNally, much to his chagrin. 'I felt I earned the respect of the players at Chester yet I was released over the phone by McNally. His attitude stinks,' Coy told me at the time.

After leaving the Cobblers, Coy turned out for Aylesbury during their one season in the GM Vauxhall Conference in 1988-89 before settling down to life as a sales representative in Redditch and indulging in his love of scuba diving, which once produced a close encounter with a shark in Egypt.

Rochdale's Spotland ground was the Cobblers' next port of call on the Saturday afternoon, where goals by Benjamin and Phil Chard – a belter of a thumping header – secured a 2-1 win.

Spotland was another venue which had proved singularly depressing for Cobblers' fans of the 1970s and 80s up to this point, only one victory and six defeats preceding this match in nine visits trailing back to 1977-78. I particularly recall standing on the terraces there for a 3-5 defeat in the final month of the 1981-82 season when the Cobblers were heading for re-election. I even managed to miss Mark Heeley's Cobblers opener in the first few minutes as I stayed too long in the Cemetery pub.

The Cobblers faced Division Four's leading 1985-86 scorer Steve Taylor on this particular afternoon, but although he cancelled out Benjamin's opener, a far-post scissor-kick from a Morley cross, Chard's ghost-like run to meet Coy's free-kick with a bullet header midway through the second period earned the spoils. Chard said: 'It was very off the cuff and unrehearsed. It became evident during the game that the back-post area was clear and I asked Bobby whether he could hit it and he did just that.'

It still wasn't enough to take the Cobblers to the top of Division Four, but the moment wasn't long in coming against local rivals Peterborough in a Sunday match which featured a classic number of reunions, with ex-Posh men Chard and Benjamin pitted against ex-Cobblers Wakeley Gage and Derrick Christie in the visitors' line-up.

It was heart-warming to see Christie back at the County Ground for his first match since a 2-2 draw with Stockport in 1978. His career had subsequently taken him to Cambridge, Reading and Cardiff before moving to London Road. Those of a certain age still recall his habitual pre-match ritual of juggling footballs along the passage behind the Hotel End to the Wantage Road exit.

Still, Christie was helpless to prevent the new wave from powering on, goals from Morley and a Chard penalty ensuring Dave Gregory's late consolation was largely academic in front of what match correspondent Brian Barron described as: 'A Division One table-topping crowd if your club is Wimbledon.'

The 2-0 win over Tranmere three days later took Carr's men back to the top just 24 hours after Preston had defeated Halifax in a five-goal thriller, Jon Thomas bagging a hat-trick from 0-2 down at half-time, one of three hat-tricks he would score during the course of the season. The Cobblers' victory prompted Carr to comment: 'the team are playing their part – I hope the fans can carry on theirs.'

The Tranmere victory was carved out thanks to an early McGoldrick strike as the Cobblers established a sort of 'poor man's Liverpool' reputation by snapping away at their opponents and always creating something, just when the contest threatened to lapse back into the mediocre.

Chard's ability to adapt – adjusting to his left-back role to keep Johnny Morrissey quiet – typified a resolute Cobblers' display rounded off by Hill's late strike when he made 'panther-like' strides onto Donald's pass before firing past Billy O'Rourke.

Swansea became the first of the sides relegated from Division Three in 1985-86 to face Carr's men the following Saturday, Lincoln, Cardiff and Wolves having been the others to drop down. It is fair to say this was something of a bleak time for Welsh football, given the Swans' financial problems. It was ironic that Newport County, who only narrowly avoided making it a hat-trick of relegated Welsh clubs, by finishing in nineteenth place, should be regarded as the Red Dragon 'elite' at this time.

Swansea had appointed Terry Yorath as their manager on 19 July, just nine days before a High Court winding up order imposed the previous December, had finally been lifted.

Both sides had a boost going into the contest, for Preston's authority as leaders had been shattered by a first defeat of the season, 0-4 at Scunthorpe on the Friday evening, Steve Lister getting a pair, Billy Russell and Julian Broddle the others. However, the Cobblers soon joined the Lilywhites in casting off their unbeaten tag, leaving Swansea, Cambridge and Exeter to carry on flying this flag.

Swansea's own rise and fall to Division One and back to the basement had been as meteoric as the Cobblers' own 1960s exploits. Finishing third to Graham Taylor's Watford in Division Four in 1977-78, they reached Division One in 1981, gaining promotion thanks to a 3-1 win over Preston. By 1986 though, it was back to square one.

On a warm September afternoon which coincided with Richard Hill's 23rd birthday, the Cobblers succumbed to defeat despite another Chard header, this time a near-post effort from a Dave Gilbert corner. It sandwiched goals by Sean McCarthy and Ian Love after the Cobblers' defence was twice outdone by simple crosses from veteran winger Tommy Hutchison, best remembered for a long career with Coventry and scoring for both sides in the 1981 FA Cup final when he played for Manchester City against Spurs, the latter winning after a replay.

It briefly seemed that some of the Cobblers' early-season enthusiasm might have subsided at Swansea, the balloon cynically popped, although in the *Chronicle & Echo* Brian Barron reported on a fiercely competitive contest which produced tremendous football. His closing speculation had a persuasive ring: 'The fans could well have been watching this season's Fourth Division champions.'

Barron had never been a man averse to a punt during his life, and on this occasion he proved completely spot on.

CHAPTER FOUR

Murder on the (Leyton) Orient Express

I've often wondered which of the numerous Agatha Christie titles Alan Carr was reading as he sat with a thoughtful expression on his brow in the Cobblers' Meccano Stand during the October and spring half-term holidays during 1986-87. Grudging agreement to tag along with dad to work didn't quite help to produce the expected career outcome. Or perhaps it did. Humour, after all, can be found anywhere, in a multitude of situations, or from reading detective novels come to that.

Dame Agatha Christie penned around 80 of that genre, mostly featuring either her famous Belgian detective, Hercule Poirot, or the spinster of St Mary Mead, Jane Marple.

However, if my memory serves me correctly, neither appeared in 'N or M?' which may have had the search for a German wartime spy at a south coast hotel theme, or it may simply have referred to Nebbeling or McPherson? – the quandary concerning exactly which centre-half Carr senior should have signed on loan during 1985-86 to play alongside Russell Lewis in the heart of the defence.

'Why Didn't They Ask Evans?' is another cryptic poser easily ticked off the Cobblers' 'Whodunnit?' list. In the Christie book the answer lies in the fact that Evans is the maiden name of the parlour maid who would have recognised some skulduggery had she been asked to witness a will. So she wasn't. Cobblers fans know that the reason no one asked Dr John Evans to initially switch across from Nuneaton to be club secretary was that the club had already pilfered everybody else from that part of the Midlands who was any use to anybody, and were trying to spread the load for a little while.

We could go on (and briefly will). 'Endless Night' refers to the four minutes of injury-time on the night the Cobblers clinched the Division Four title against Crewe, 'Death in the Clouds' was a cynical reference to the long-ball game penned by jealous opposition; while 'The 4.50 from Paddington' can easily be reverted to 'The 9.42 to Oblivion' – a subtle reference to the Cobblers' lowest ever gate against Chester in March 1985, and the club's subsequent grim prospects of survival.

However, the Cobblers were not alone in aligning their fortunes to Christie titles during the 1980s. Mighty Wolves had suffered their own version of Three Act Tragedy by being relegated in consecutive years – 1983-84 from Division One. The following season Wolves plunged from

Division Two, before entering the League's basement for the first time after dropping from Division Three in 1985-86.

Reference to the 1944 Christie novel *Towards Zero* also seems appropriate with its sliding connotations, even though Superintendent Battle had been faced by a handsome tennis player in the form of Nevile Strange, rather than a wartime professional footballer in his task of unmasking the killer of Lady Tresilian at Gull's Point. In all honesty the latter would have been a much better name for Torquay's ground than Plainmoor.

Detective fantasy aligned to Cobblers' matches later spread to the Arthur Conan-Doyle and Sherlock Holmes league on 18 April 1992 when Phil Chard's team was beaten 1-2 at Carlisle. It might have been far from elementary, but the home goals were supplied by Mick Holmes and Andrew Watson, who had apparently succeeded Dr Watson by then. 'Clueless!' would have been a good headline in the *Chron*, but I don't think it would have either been fair on the side at the time, or indeed was used. Holmes, however, was a player Chard had known from his Wolves days and whom he signed the following season. He probably also remembered that when the Cobblers drew the return match 1-1 at Wolves in February 1987, they had both been on the scoresheet.

Speaking of Chard, I always had a secret desire to write a headline which read 'Singed not Chard' or even 'Chard remains'. The former could have been appropriate to a rampant Cobblers performance on a baking hot day when the side were just edged out, with the latter fitting the bill after a failed transfer bid. Somehow the opportunity never arose, although 'Chard fillip for Cobblers' made a show in the *Sports Pink 'Un* after the 2-1 win at Rochdale in September.

There is a fine line to be drawn when interlacing humour with tragedy, but we are all aware it has become part of the English culture, whether rightly or wrongly. Tragedy certainly struck on the night of 10 September 1985 when Scotland manager Jock Stein died of a heart attack in the medical room at Ninian Park after his country's 1-1 draw with Wales had earned them a play-off against Australia, which ultimately led to qualification to the next year's World Cup in Mexico. Stein's assistant that night was one Alex Ferguson, whose lengthy stretch as manager at Manchester United began in early November 1986.

On the same evening, the Cobblers were hammering Preston 6-0 at the County Ground, the sort of result capable of registering shockwaves throughout the British Isles. When the terrible news filtered through from Cardiff, the point was made in the pokey Northampton dressing room. How much responsibility must we take for our actions?

Aidy Mann, Graham Carr, Russell Wilcox, Clive Walker, Mark Bushell and Denis Casey take stock of the situation at Rochdale (September 1986)

David Gilbert jinks his way past Exeter's Brendon O'Connell during the 1-1 draw at St James Park (January 1987)

The County Ground is no place for an Agatha Christie novel, so Graham Carr shows son Alan (right) the way to the dressing room before the 3-0 win over Cambridge. The lad in the middle is Spencer Lambert (March 1987)

Who ate all the pies? Graham Reed and Trevor Morley indulge in their favourite take-aways on the way home from Tranmere (February 1987)

CHAMPAGNE COBBLERS 1986-87

Exeter goalkeeper John Shaw tips a Hill header onto the crossbar at the other St James Park (January 1987)

Cobblers skipper Trevor Morley makes an aerial connection with Crewe's Peter Billing on the title-winning night (April 1987)

Can you keep the noise down please? A more refined brand of football fan was being moulded at the County Ground (February 1987)

Richard Hill salutes another goal, this time in the 4-4 FA Cup draw at Southend (December 1986)

Richard Hill buries a header in the 5-0 romp against Crewe at Gresty Road
(November 1986)

Trevor Morley working in the treatment room under the watchful eye of physio Denis
Casey after suffering his knee injury in the FA Cup-tie at Newcastle (January 1987)

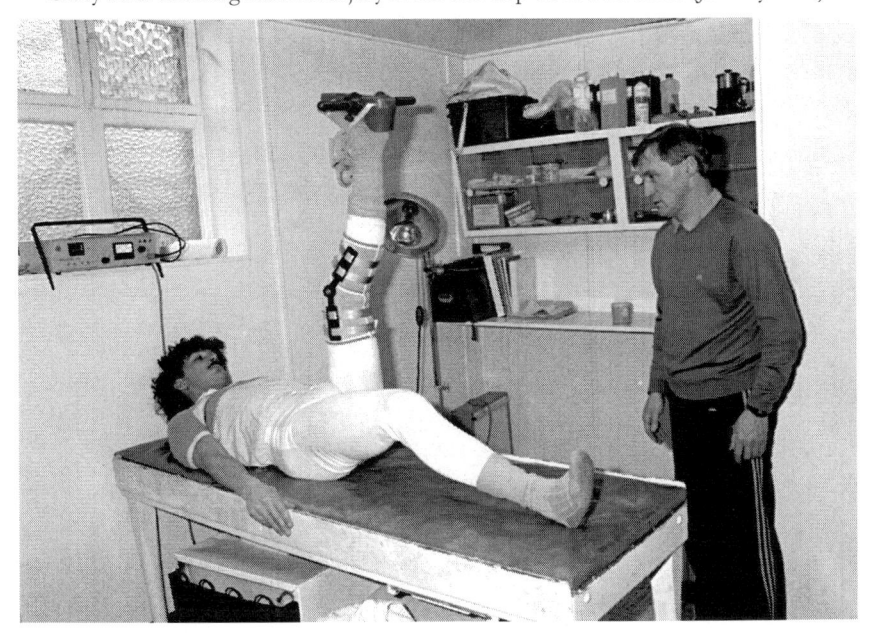

Midfield dynamo Warren Donald gets stuck in against Leyton Orient's Alan Comfort, who is today the club chaplain at Brisbane Road The O's Chris Jones looks on (April 1987)

Richard Hill is surrounded by a posse of Hartlepool players in the 3-3 draw at the Victoria Ground. Notice the Portakabin changing rooms (November 1986)

Aldershot's Glen Burvill is sent off by referee Vanes as future Cobbler Bobby Barnes (centre) leads the remonstrations in the 3-3 draw at the Recreation Ground (May 1987)

Cobblers chairman and tobacco businessman Derek Banks had been burning the candle at both ends before returning from the 5-0 win at Crewe (November 1986)

Ian Benjamin performs his party-piece nutmeg against Peterborough's Wakeley Gage just seconds before curling home the winner at London Road (January 1987)

Can you come back at 5pm? A return ticket on a helicopter is briefly on offer before the 3-0 FA Cup victory over Peterborough (November 1986)

With Scunthorpe's Richard Money grounded, Richard Hill turns to celebrate with Keith McPherson after getting the new season off to a great start after five minutes (August 1986)

The new season is only ten minutes old and the Cobblers are already 2-0 up at Scunthorpe, as Graham Reed's header flies into the top corner (August 1986)

Dave Gilbert is in urgent need of recovery time after the 1-1 draw at Tranmere (February 1987)

Manager Graham Carr can always find time to celebrate, and does so with sons Gary and Alan prior to the title-clinching win over Crewe at the County Ground (April 1987)

Champagne Cobblers 1986-87

Newcastle here we come! Cobblers players Peter Gleasure, Graham Reed, Keith Gorman, Aidy Mann, Richard Hill and Eddie McGoldrick in the team bath after the 3-2 FA Cup replay success against Southend (December 1986)

Fans had to be patient prior to the Christmas home fixture with Cardiff City, lining the route along Abington Avenue (December 1986)

Silencing the Gallowgate roar. Richard Hill's equaliser at Newcastle raises brief hopes of a fourth round FA Cup date (January 1987)

Cobblers players (from left) Dave Logan, Trevor Morley, Peter Gleasure, Ian Benjamin, Dave Gilbert and Bobby Coy take to Abington Park on the Sunday after the match at Hereford is called off (March 1987)

Eddie McGoldrick scored in both games against Lincoln. In the home match he directs his effort between a ruck of defenders into the Hotel End goal (December 1986)

An airborne Ian Benjamin converts a chip over Rochdale goalkeeper Dave Redfern for the opener at Spotland in the 2-1 win (September 1986)

Cobblers players thank the County Ground faithful for their support, prior to the 2-1 victory over Crewe which clinched the Today League Division Four title (April 1987)

An anguished Trevor Morley faced a six week absence after injuring his knee in the 2-1 FA Cup defeat at Newcastle. Concerned team-mates look on (January 1987)

Cobblers' defender Graham Reed endures the pain barrier during summer pre-season training at Northampton's British Timken Sports Ground (July 1986)

Eddie McGoldrick and Torquay goalkeeper John Smeulders are set to collide in the first home game of the season at the County Ground (August 1986)

The Cobblers' Russell Wilcox and Wolves' David Barnes in direct opposition during the 1-1 draw at Molineux (February 1987)

Cobblers' players indulge in premature celebrations with chairman Derek Banks and the management team after the 2-1 win over Stockport at the County Ground (March 1987)

This coincidence would have been bad enough, but the tale broadened 32 days later when Carr took his side to Peterborough for the 5-0 execution of the local rivals. Taking up the story he recalled: 'We were halfway home between Thrapston and Finedon when we saw a car on fire in a field. The reaction of the lads was that the driver had probably been happily driving along when he heard the classified football results on the radio causing him to drive off the road.'

The fact remains that even if you didn't set fire to your car or throw yourself from a bridge, no one could quite believe what was happening at that time with Carr's team, who might have been Cobblers by name, though certainly not in performance.

Yet it was ironic rather than hysterical that all three clubs who had all partaken of the Division One to Division Four roller-coaster adventure – Swansea, Wolves and the Cobblers – should meet within the space of a month at this time. The Swans scored a 1-0 win over Wolves at the Vetch Field on 18 October.

The 2-1 victory at the expense of the Old Gold shirts was a notable scalp for Carr's men, whatever the visitors' problems during the brief tenure of Brian Little (he was replaced by Graham Turner the following month). It was a stand-out victory against a historic club who were a shadow of the giant which had won the League three times and the FA Cup twice from 1949-1970.

The last County Ground meeting between the clubs had been almost twenty years earlier, when the Old Gold shirts had triumphed 4-0 in the year the Cobblers dropped into Division Two. Clive Walker wore the Cobblers' No 3 shirt that afternoon, although there were a number of other curious links.

It was a season Wolves were promoted back to Division One, with the Cobblers sliding in the other direction, but three of the Wolves goals – his only hat-trick for the club – were netted by Ernie Hunt, who later made history at Coventry along with Willie Carr for the famous 'donkey kick' goal against Everton that was then outlawed. Wolves also included Mike Bailey, who applied for the Cobblers' managerial post in 1984 when Tony Barton was successful, along with goalkeeper Fred Davies who was coach alongside John Bond when the Cobblers won their nail-biting survival match to stay in the Football League. They won 3-2 at Shrewsbury in 1993 at the expense of Halifax. Surely Chard's finest hour, as the side rallied from 0-2 down at half-time.

Briefly, at least, the roles were reversed on that September afternoon in 1986. Morley and Hill gave the Cobblers a half-time lead which survived a severe second-half examination, although Andy Mutch headed a goal from Dean Edwards' cross. Birmingham loanee Ian Handysides was behind most of Wolves' best efforts.

At least, as far as Wolves supporters were concerned, their period in the doldrums was not extended and they won titles in consecutive years, 1988 and 1989. It meant a more upbeat end to a decade which had opened with them triumphing in the 1980 League Cup final under John Barnwell when they beat holders and European Cup champions Nottingham Forest 1-0 with a goal by Andy Gray.

The Barnwell connection is another curious offshoot of the period as the Cobblers were the last league club he managed from 1993-94, succeeding none other than Chard in that post. The pair's careers had crossed much earlier, while Barnwell had also played against the Cobblers three times for Forest in Division One during 1965-66, twice in the league and once in the FA Cup.

Ironically, Forest and Wolves were also clubs to appear on the career of Corby-born Chard, who was at the City Ground at the same time as Gary Mills, later to win a European Cup-winners medal there. Then, both Chard and Mills were playing for Northants schoolboys, before Chard spent three months at Coventry during the Gordon Milne era (also Ernie Hunt and Willie Carr), switching to Peterborough under Barnwell. Chard was still in the sixth form at Corby and recollected combining studies with playing in the reserves at London Road.

He said: 'I remember being due to make my first-team debut for Peterborough when Irish international Trevor Anderson was injured and John wanted me to play up front off Barry Butlin. Unfortunately he went down with flu and it changed the plan.'

Although Barnwell went off to replace Sammy Chung at the helm at Wolves, Chard spent seven years at London Road between 1978-85 under managers such as the ex-Cobblers winger Billy Hails, Peter Morris, Martin Wilkinson and finally John Wile, at a time when Ian Benjamin was also at the club.

Chard made his Posh debut as a substitute against Swindon, his first start in a 1-1 draw with Rotherham, and his first goal in a 3-0 home win over Hull, all late in the 1978-79 season. Posh were relegated from Division Three that season, but he recalled: 'It was remarkable, as Micky Gynn, Tony Cliss and myself were all young trainees who had come through the youth set up, and who all scored that day.'

Feeling fortunate to be in a Peterborough side boasting a decent youth base, Chard blossomed alongside players such as Gynn and future Cobbler Trevor Quow. He was also lucky in his local derby deals in Cobblers v Peterborough matches, like Benjamin switching sides at just the right time as the balance of power in East Anglia shifted from London Road to the County Ground, a little like a latter-day Warwick the Kingmaker during the War of the Roses.

Chard didn't play in the dismal (for Northampton supporters) 1981 FA Cup-tie which Posh won 4-1 at the County Ground, salt being rubbed into the wounds as the goals all came from past or future Northampton links – Tommy Robson (two), Trevor Slack and Trevor Quow – but like Benjamin he found the net in the first year of the Football League Trophy in 1982-83, Benjamin helping himself to a double while Slack and Robbie Cooke also hit the target in a 5-2 success at London Road.

Chard's switch to the mediocre surroundings of the County Ground was far from a racing certainty, especially given his local upbringing. He said: 'As a Corby lad I knew all about the place with its three sides, and didn't think I would ever play there. But it was Graham Carr who sold it to me when I met him. He was so enthusiastic and motivated. He had a plan and knew what he wanted to achieve. In fact he was a real player's manager.'

Benjamin and Chard were also on the scoresheet when the Cobblers travelled to the Old Shay Ground three days after the Wolves victory. Mind you, as the outcome was a 6-3 victory, that's hardly surprising. At first glance you might assume any player who fancied a goal simply helped himself to the opportunity. In fact Hill's third hat-trick for the Cobblers meant this wasn't the case. Hill recalled: 'That was the night our director Martin Pell told me he would give me a leather jacket if I scored a hat-trick, as he was in that line of business, but I don't think he was too impressed when it happened!'

'Rampant Richard far from over the hill,' screamed the *Chron* headline for the report of the game. In fact, it had only been just over four and a half years since the club's last contest involving at least nine goals, a 3-7 defeat at Sheffield United. However, they haven't had one since, although Hill managed to trump that during his time later on with Oxford United, when he scored in a Division Two match at Luton on the plastic pitch which was lost 4-7. He recalled: 'That was the craziest match I ever played in and there was a picture of our goalkeeper Steve Hardwick standing with his hands on his hips after letting the last goal in – the clock behind him stood at 4.20pm. It was the days when matches actually finished at 4.40pm so there were still 20 minutes to go!'

Halifax looked easy pickings going into the clash, despite the fact that Cobblers sides had lost four and drawn one of their five previous visits there. Let's face it, as I glance back at my match programme, they couldn't even get the correct month on the cover, claiming it was already 30

October. With that, subsequent events and the usual low-key atmosphere at a ground where the pitch was surrounded by a speedway track, it made for a surreal night.

My own recollections surround the presence in the press-box of my lifelong friend and mutual best man Chris Barritt, whose enthusiasm for football and involvement on the media side of the fence, was only matched at the time by his passion for local tennis.

Chris and I travelled to the match together as, for once, photographer Norton was sidelined. Unfortunately, though, I had not had sufficient chance to brief my new companion on press-box etiquette – the type of 'dos and don'ts' if your team happen to score, perhaps once and maybe twice if you were lucky. The sort of pumped up adrenalin normally saved for a blockbuster cross-court forehand winner or a ferocious smash at the net, you know the sort of thing – punching the air and screaming at the man next to you – is just not quite *de rigeur* when the guy from the *Yorkshire Post* is squatting alongside you on the bench. Remember, you are engaged on a serious professional assignment and, however miserable your press-box colleagues might appear to be, you are not under any account allowed to wind them up during the game.

Instead, it is better to thoughtfully chew or suck your pencil (I remember pencils and crayons, as I was a child of the 1960s) and then pretend to check a minor detail in the build-up to the goal with said YP hack, such as: 'Was that the No 6 Galloway who slipped awkwardly on his backside before Hill lashed the ball home from twelve yards?'

Unfortunately, as you might gather, the message did not truly get across to Chris and I spent an uncomfortable evening squirming with embarrassment as the goals rained in and my sidekick made the most of his night out by showing his colours.

Looking back on the Halifax spectacle, it seems incredible now that my piece was angled on a disappointing defensive display when the side had bagged six on their travels, something the club had not achieved in the league for over 55 years (6-2 at Walsall) and have not done since, although they did manage an 8-1 win at Peterborough in the FA Cup in December 1946, the sort of result which tends to allow you forgiveness for the odd 60 or so years of inconsistency. Yet there was still a genuine sense of anti-climax at Halifax that the home team had pulled it back to 5-3 with 21 minutes left.

That image, the classic Hill and Morley celebration shot, was snapped during the next game on the agenda, the 4-2 win over Aldershot four days later. Manager Carr had also won his first Manager of the Month award that season for the side's September form, the other divisional accolades going to Brian Clough (Nottingham Forest), Alan Ball (Portsmouth) and Bruce Rioch (Middlesbrough). Yet once again I found myself taking the alternative view and news angle – Chard again.

The headline in the *Chron* on the Monday read: 'Phil knocks resistance on the head,' a reference to the fact the utility man had packed much into his afternoon's endeavours – a missed penalty, a near substitution when he refused to come off after being virtually knocked out cold, before (surprise, surprise) scoring a crucial goal to put the Cobblers ahead. That was real *Roy of the Rovers* stuff, and so was the Norton picture that came after Hill's towering header from McGoldrick's 78th-minute cross.

That goal concluded the scoring and the snapper recalled: 'I was sitting in my usual position by the Hotel End goal, close to where the goal line and the 18-yard box line met. Most of the pictures I took after that goal had the celebrating players with their back to me but there was just the one frame where they turned. It just turned out to be the iconic shot of that season – a piece of luck.'

Showman Hill was soon to learn the lesson of playing to the Hotel End audience, while also acquiring an awareness of where the camera was. At one point he asked Norton why he never took the feted 'punch the air' shots to which the photographer replied: 'Well, you never run towards me.'

From that point on, the situation was rectified, a case of 'you scratch my back and I'll scratch yours'. The Burnley game, soon afterwards, began a trend of 'nod as good as a wink' type situations at corners, where Hill would make eye contact with Norton and suggest something was about to happen.

Chard, though, shared the headlines against The Shots, experiencing a bizarre afternoon as he saw his first-half spot-kick brilliantly pushed away by Tony Lange before being poleaxed in the second and almost being counted out. It even got as far as the County Ground tannoy announcing he had been substituted, although he was having none of it. Perhaps with the blow to the head he had forgotten where he was.

It is worth recalling that the Cobblers' season masked a superb one for the Shots, who ultimately earned promotion via the end of season roulette at the expense of Wolves. They had finished nine points behind Wolves in the league, Carr recalling watching the Old Golds comprehensively beat Len Walker's side 3-0 in the league at Molineux. Yet it counted for nothing when future Cobbler Bobby Barnes scored the home goal to round off a 3-0 aggregate final win after Phil Neal's Bolton had been beaten by Aldershot in the semi-finals (ex-Cobbler and Liverpool hero Neal guided Bolton back up to Division Three at the first attempt).

In a dramatic season for Aldershot, they also knocked First Division Oxford United out of the FA Cup 3-0 in the third round before losing to Barnsley after a replay. They also reached the Southern final of the Freight Rover Trophy, where they lost to beaten finalists Bristol City (Mansfield winning the final on penalties). Football anoraks love the fact that Aldershot defeated Fulham 11-10 in a 22-penalty, Area quarter-final shoot-out.

The league contest with The Shots was a superb early advert for the *Today* newspaper, which two days earlier had emerged as the Football League's new sponsor in a £4 million deal over two years. The Cobblers showed the sort of steamroller power which allowed them to eventually grind down opposition, something Chard alluded to when he remarked: 'The clues were there the year before when you could see the side were going to carry on that impetus. Even when we were behind you always felt we were going to push on and win matches in the final 20 minutes.'

The Aldershot match was also among the first which Carr's old 1960s playing colleague Jim Hall stepped in to assist Mike Cox on the Northampton Hospital Radio service. In the circumstances it was hardly surprising that he made reference to the relative lack of experience in the line-up. There were no old heads in the Cobblers' side, with players such as Chard, Gleasure and Benjamin being among the most senior. Chard was the oldest, yet he had not turned 26 at the onset of 1986-87.

Stockport should have been the side's next opponents, but the scheduled 11 October date was put back sixteen days due to illness in the Edgeley Park camp. This naturally left Carr frustrated and angry, understandably viewing the 'crying off' by The Hatters as a lame excuse. Stockport had crashed 0-5 at Cambridge on the previous Friday night, spectacularly capitulated 0-7 at home to Sheffield Wednesday three days later in the second leg of their second round Littlewoods Cup tie (0-10 on aggregate) and were in the middle of a twelve-match run which saw two draws and ten losses. It even culminated in a first-round FA Cup exit at Caernarfon Town. It begged the question: 'Would you naturally want to play the runaway league leaders at this time?'

Suffice to say, Stockport were not in good shape when the Cobblers went to Edgeley Park and won 3-0, although in the meantime there was the small matter of the 3-2 local derby success at Cambridge on a Friday night – earned with goals by Keith McPherson, his first for the club, a Chard penalty, and Morley – along with home dates against Burnley and Hereford.

The Cambridge match was also significant for bringing the first change to the league starting line-up at the tenth time of asking. Russell

Wilcox came in to partner McPherson at the heart of the defence, at the expense of Bobby Coy. Wilcox, signed from Frickley in the summer, had suffered a frustrating start to life at Northampton after suffering a knee injury in pre-season, but he had been gently eased in, making a substitute appearance at home to Wolves.

McPherson had played against the Cobblers the season before while on loan at Cambridge, in a match Carr's men won 5-2, and the evening paid further testimony to the side's durability, as they trailed at the break for the second match in a row. It is also worth reflecting that this was only Cambridge's second defeat of any description at that stage, having gone down 0-1 to Preston six days earlier, and the following week they knocked East Anglian rivals Ipswich out of the Littlewoods Cup. Mind you, they had drawn six Division Four matches on the trot before hammering Stockport and losing to Preston.

Morley's match-winner, twenty minutes from time, was a real gem, all the more remarkable when you consider he had notched one of similar quality at the Abbey the previous November. On this occasion he collected a screw-back from Reed, who had robbed Lindsey Smith, before picking his spot with an exquisite left-foot shot into the top corner. It was enough to send a 2,000 Cobblers' following home deliriously happy.

The boot was on the other foot on the following Wednesday night when a frenzied first-half assault brought a 3-0 lead which, to their credit, mid-table Burnley did their best to redress after the break. The Clarets hit back with goals by Leighton James and Ashley Hoskin, although the final consolation only arrived five minutes from time – the Cobblers running out 4-2 winners.

Despite the fact a glut of chances were created and missed at regular intervals, the Cobblers stretched their lead to seven points. It was a night for the Cobblers' goalscoring heavyweights, with Hill taking his season's tally to nine, Morley's double marching him on to six, while Benjamin now had five in league and cup. Imagine that, already twenty goals from your chief providers in thirteen matches. A manager's dream.

It was the first time that Morley had ever scored more than once in a game for Northampton, and his second saw him slam home a rebound with two defenders on the line, after Hill's chip had come back off the crossbar. Benjamin's strike was a rasping back-post volley from Donald's cross.

Certain song lyrics have a curious habit of recurring in my head when fondly remembering my match-reporting days, and at this moment the 1976 Paul Simon hit *Fifty Ways To Leave Your Lover* springs to mind. Why so? Simply that as an old news reporting colleague Simon Redley used to remark when I had done something daft: 'That's a funny way of handing in your resignation!'

Hence the fact that the words: 'You just slip out the back, Jack, make a new plan Stan, no need to be coy Roy' (or in the Cobblers case should that have been 'Roy, Coy?'), just get yourself free' come into my head at this point. For by switching the 'lover' part to job departure, the analogy became more obvious when considering the Hereford match. Although it never actually came to the crunch, my performance against The Bulls suggested I seemed to be seriously examining my choice of exit doors from the *Chron*.

The occasion was manager Carr's birthday party at home to Hereford. His arrival at 42 neatly coincided with his gallon bottle of scotch award from Bell's before the game, which was a well documented event. Less well publicised was the fact he should have also received a celebratory birthday cake courtesy of the *Chronicle & Echo*, planned by the thoughtfulness of newspaper editor Green. The idea was to make the presentation before the game, but thanks to yours truly, it never happened.

In later years, when considering a change of careers, it never occurred to me to entertain the notion of confectionary conveyance, and with very good reason. Charged with what in hindsight seemed the simple task of collecting the boxed item from Oliver Adams in the town and delivering it to the County Ground, I failed miserably in my task. Examining the contents of the cake on arrival at the County Ground at my usual 1.30pm, I discovered a mass of scrunched up icing and crumbs which, while doubtless still tasty, would have had you believe it had been transported across the Mediterranean during a particularly rough crossing, rather than the length of Abington Avenue in a carrier bag.

Boss Carr was suitably sympathetic. Perhaps he secretly didn't fancy it anyway (watching the figure and all that) and I'm sure it wouldn't have gone down too well as an accompaniment to scotch. Meanwhile, back at Upper Mounts, editor Green kept his thoughts to himself, and I pressed on, determined to redeem myself. To use another baking term, the roll continued with a 3-2 victory against The Bulls. Anoraks will be impressed to learn this was one of two results during the season that were transposed when the returns were later played on (the 3-1 home win and loss at Lincoln being the other).

Contrary to the popularly held theory that the Cobblers gradually ground down opponents the longer a game wore on, the opposite held true here, for the side led 3-0 at half-time. In fact, with goals by Morley and Benjamin for the second match running, both in the first eight minutes, it really seemed as though the birthday party had been arranged for half-time. Hill was also on target, which meant he hit double figures for the season and was joint top-scorer in the section at this stage.

However, judging by The Bulls' storming second half, perhaps the Cobblers did start early on the messed-up confection. At any rate, with the wind at their backs, Stewart Phillips and Steve Devine made it 3-2 and only the linesman's flag prevented Phillips' apparent late equaliser from being allowed to stand.

Forty-eight hours later the Cobblers' points tally reached 34, and more significantly, a lead of ten points, after Stockport were put to the sword 3-0 at Edgeley Park on a night when Carr was sent to the stands by referee Watson after a string of strong words to a linesman.

Such was the nature of his bellowing and decibel count that night, that the simple process of moving back a few feet had little effect at an eerie Stockport ground. Something of a pointless exercise really – while Hill's double either side of half-time set up the victory with Morley's late effort completing the job against the hapless Hatters.

Seven straight victories put the side on the brink of a club record – the eight achieved by Dave Bowen's team in Division Four between 27 August and 19 September 1960, when they began with a 2-1 win over Aldershot and ended with a 3-2 success against Chester, scoring 24 goals in the process.

The seven consecutive wins in 1986-87 brought one more goal than that, but the chance to match those earlier exploits was blown away on a farcical afternoon at 'a wretched' Victoria Ground at Hartlepool where the wind and rain blew in from the North Sea in copious and random quantity.

Changing in the Portakabin at Hartlepool had been a regular feature for many years – after all, Pool were the division's longest servers at that time, and cash had never been theirs to burn. Since the creation of Division Four in 1958, Hartlepool had spent all bar one season (1968-69) employed in football's basement, so this experience was surely the true essence of Division Four football.

It was a day for severing other records that day, notably at Exeter, who surrendered the Football League's last unbeaten record on 1 November. Their 1-2 loss at Preston, going down to an Andy McAteer goal in the 89th minute, meant they dropped from third to sixth in the table after drawing eight of their opening thirteen Division Four matches that season. Peterborough parted company with their manager John Wile, before their 0-0 draw at Burnley on that afternoon.

Hartlepool were the only Division Four side that season apart from Swansea not to lose to the Cobblers in 1986-87 and Roy Hogan was on target early on as the sides swapped penalties – Hogan was also the guilty handball party as Chard levelled matters up.

The Cobblers led for only two minutes that afternoon, and it needed Hill's second of the game, which made him the Football League's top scorer with fourteen, to earn a 3-3 share of the spoils.

My report on the match related how a booking for Chard meant he would miss the first round round FA Cup-tie with his old club Peterborough just fifteen days later, with Donald starting a three-match ban at the same time. It would now be a case of riding the storm and applying the 'Liverpool' technique of grinding out results in less than ideal conditions. 'Donald was one of several Cobblers "touch players" to struggle in the mud at Hartlepool's bleak home, a goal-kick from the North Sea, and for all the fluency the game had, they might just as well have played in it.'

At least, though, the unbeaten run was preserved, setting the side up nicely for the trip to London on the following Tuesday night and a meeting with Leyton Orient.

Headline writers on the *Chronicle & Echo* sports desk often indulged a whimsical sense of humour when appropriate occasions rose – causing a good deal of mirth and merriment over the years among Cobblers supporters. The trip to Brisbane Road was a case in point. The following evening's match report of 'Leyton Orient 0, Northampton Town 1' in the *Chron* brought an immortal piece of Dave Hickey subbing. Surely only he could have come up with 'Super cool "Benji" finds the chink in Orient', although I'm not sure it would have been allowed in these days of unilateral harmony.

Moments like this always led me to nostalgically look back on vintage football headlines. I have already reflected on the potential of matches against Crewe, including 'no change' and 'cuts', but that still leaves old favourites such as Hereford 1 Northampton 1 – 'Bulls held by the Cobblers'. It was also appropriate that the 7-1 hammering of Bristol City in September 1982 had been played on the Sabbath and presented the opportunity for 'Seventh Heaven'.

Perhaps, though, my favourite tale in this domain is the one with which colleague Brian Barron used to regale once I had deigned to purchase a round of morning coffees from the machine (a disgusting 37 – white, no sugar) as we sighed collective relief all round in the wake of an early edition deadline.

The match at the centre of focus took place on a Friday night, 28 February 1975 and brought the scoreline, Northampton 0 Reading 3. Apparently, the Cobblers had proved more than a match for the

Biscuitmen for most of the evening, only to succumb to sucker punches on the break – a familiar scenario for many who recall the age. Barron portrayed as much in his match report, only to be dismayed the following day when the early edition ran with the heading: 'Despite score, Cobblers superb' which he felt was stretching credibility a little bit too far. Clearly they were not superb at all.

Although it was hurriedly changed for the final edition, a luxury not available nowadays, that wasn't the end of the story as Barron related. 'All the football writers from United Newspapers used to converge in the London office at the end of the season on FA Cup final day for a drink, before going on to cover the game for their papers.

'That year I went to the West Ham v Fulham final but on arrival discovered a cutting with that ridiculous headline pinned up on the wall. I was so embarrassed I spent most of the next hour having a drink with my back to that wall so nobody brought attention to it.'

Back at Brisbane Road, I recall the night for several other events – the match was played on 4 November, which meant the skies were alive with pre-Bonfire Night colour as yours truly, the named chauffeur into northeast London on the night, was charged with delivering the Northampton press gang to the game on time, not something with which I had 100 per cent success over the season.

My concentration levels were at their most intense, as my car full of freelance journalist Mike Berry, Chris Barritt and photographer Pete Norton neared the destination. However, my senses can't have been that hot – when I thought we were getting close, I suggested pulling the car over and asking a local for directions. 'I recognise that block of flats – I'm sure it's not far from here,' said an encouraging Norton.

Winding the window down, Barritt spotted a passer-by who turned out to be postman. Ideal! 'Where's the ground, mate?' I asked the man in the Royal Mail uniform. Instead of looking down the street as I expected, he simply stopped and adjusted his gaze vertically. 'Just up there,' he replied, pointing upwards with a gesture which could have been misinterpreted as a rude one less than ten years later. Once everyone else in the car had stopped laughing, I craned my neck to inspect more closely, and there sure enough, was one of the Brisbane Road floodlights.

We hastily parked and clicked into match mode, with the contest won early on. All in all, it proved something of a surreal night. One angle on the occasion was the fact the TNT Ipec sponsorship emblazoned on the Cobblers' shirts did not curry favour with the locals – this was the era of the Wapping dispute involving around 6,000 journalists at a time when newspapers were being moved away from their historical home at Fleet

Street. TNT was the name on the newspaper lorries employed delivering and supplying Fort Wapping.

At Orient, the Cobblers won by the only goal, with leading marksman Hill turning provider. The Football League's top scorer used his devastating pace to an alternative effect after eleven minutes when he went haring off down the right wing in pursuit of Orient's John Sitton, although at the time he looked a poor second in the race for the ball. However, when Sitton dallied, Hill took it from him and pulled the ball back for Benjamin to beat Peter Wells from six yards.

No one ever claimed it was a thriller that night, but the events of the evening left me questioning many years later whether I had really become such a spoilt child. After scoring 26 goals in their previous seven league matches (never fewer than three in a game), Carr's men were in danger of making everyone a bit blasé about the roll, and the stunning way it was being executed.

I commented on the fact that recent entertainment levels had dipped, during the game's post-match press conference. It was probably asking for trouble, although a slightly tetchy Carr showed surprising reserve in reminding me it wasn't always a case of just turning up and slamming five goals past the opposition just when we fancied it. At the time he diplomatically remarked: 'It is another great performance away from home. I am very pleased,' while I added the inference in my report that he felt there was too much criticism of his side.

I justified my judgements by adding: 'The fact is that the Cobblers have set such high standards with their exciting blend of attacking football that any regular followers expect nothing less than perfection.'

It appeared a case of 'so much for the spoilt child' syndrome again. While I was perhaps due a small sigh of relief that an assassination attempt had not been made on my life, top scorer Hill had good reason to be thankful for the severely intensive training methods employed by Messrs Carr and Walker, which had created a super-fit unit capable of grinding most opposition down and running them ragged.

'It was murder,' he said.

CHAPTER FIVE

Riding a Gresty Road Wave

So precise and clinical was the progress of the Cobblers for the next seven matches that, if studied on a pathfinder map of Division Four, it almost resembled one of those World War Two underground plotting caverns situated somewhere on the south coast, probably a pebble's throw from Dover.

You know the type. I've seen them on the old black and white films starring people like Kenneth More, Sir Laurence Olivier and Trevor Howard. They're full of government officials looking down as pretty, yet diligent girls in uniform noiselessly move union jacks and swastikas around like pieces on a chess board to represent the movement of Spitfire and Messerschmitt squadrons. Every once in a while Winston Churchill (or Graham Carr in this case) would pay an operational visit to keep up morale and bark a few instructions. Everyone would listen.

For sake of any argument when applied to the Cobblers' own pre-emptive strike around this time, let's call it the east-west divide. The country is bisected down the middle with claret Subbuteo-like players on the left (or west) for Division Four games. Blue men march to the right – the Cobblers' FA Cup campaign is strictly eastern bloc, ranging initially from blue-shirted Peterborough and Southend players before eventually (in late January) sweeping up to the north-east like a rampaging weather front and resting in black and white waves around the city of Newcastle.

Preston, Crewe, Exeter and Wrexham, all leaning to the west, provided the next four league rivals. At the risk of sounding like the Reverend W Awdry and recreating *Thomas the Tank Engine* like pieces, we've already explored the geographical lay-out of the west coast main line rail rink and noted the significance of junctions which prove vital as fill-up stops for water, Chinese take-aways, and maximum point-haul potential.

Preston had slipped to fifth in Division Four after a 0-1 home defeat by Cardiff on the Tuesday evening, and a visit to the County Ground was to bring them no immediate turning point although ultimately they stayed on best of the rest behind Carr's men. Preston's biggest weapon was no secret to the Cobblers as Steve Taylor had scored for Rochdale against them two months earlier. After swapping clubs, he again hit the target, yet was on the losing side once more. The match was interesting from the Cobblers' perspective, as Irvin Gernon made his debut, unusually for him over the course of his career in the No 7 shirt, after signing on loan from

Ipswich, while it also attracted the biggest home gate (6,537) for four years – since the 0-1 home defeat by Aston Villa in the third round of the FA Cup had been inflicted by a Mark Walters goal which had won the BBC *Match of the Day*'s Goal of the Season. In those far away blinkered days, I used to convince myself it had needed 'Goal of the Season' to prevent the Cobblers winning the FA Cup (ha ha!). Meanwhile, the crowd for Preston was even bigger than the one which saw Wimbledon lose 0-1 at home to Luton in Division One that afternoon.

Gernon's career had stalled after making England schoolboy and Under-21 appearances, a double broken leg fracture one of the principle reasons. He was 23 when he arrived at Northampton for the first time and said: 'I had just come back from loan at Newcastle and was told by the Ipswich manager Bobby Ferguson that there was the manager of a Fourth Division club wanting to talk to me in the board room.'

'My initial reaction was one of shock and not wanting to drop down, but Graham Carr sold it to me. I didn't know what to expect and on the first day was a bit late travelling from Ipswich and joined in the running at Abington Park. It seemed as though we ran for 15 miles! When we had finished and went back to the County Ground, Graham covered my eyes as a joke as I hadn't had a clue what the place looked like. It was bizarre. Before my debut I remember eight lorries arriving over the far side where they were putting together a temporary stand for the Preston match, as they were expecting a big crowd. Still, we won 3-1 and I spent the next two months at the club. I went back to Ipswich as I thought something would happen there, but didn't have a problem with Northampton. Then Keith Peacock took me on loan at Gillingham where I was injured in the end of season play-off against Sunderland.'

Gernon began the Preston game at left-back but was forced to switch to centre-half when Wilcox withdrew at half-time suffering from double vision. This also allowed McGoldrick to return after missing the previous two matches through injury and Carr reflected happily on the extra width that the player provided after the break.

Benjamin opened the scoring for the Cobblers when he deftly nipped between veteran defender Sam Allardyce and Bob McNeil before jinking inside the penalty area and wrong-footing David Brown with a neat side-foot shot into the corner.

The Lillywhites equalised after Gleasure failed to hold their first attempt of the match in the final minute of the half, but second-half efforts, a McPherson header from a Gilbert free-kick and a classic Hill charge three minutes from time, when he raced through the visitors' defence and rounded Brown, completed the scoring.

Pedestrian Preston managed just one worthwhile effort in the second half and had Osher Williams sent off after firstly earning a booking for a foul on Morley, and then carrying out a similar hatchet job on Hill. The Cobblers could even afford the luxury of a Chard penalty being blazed over the crossbar nine minutes from the end.

The draw for the first round of the FA Cup had paired the Cobblers with local rivals Peterborough at the County Ground. Posh might justifiably have argued the point, but from a Cobblers perspective it could hardly have been better. Chairman Banks and director Dick Underwood added spice to the occasion by arriving on stage in a helicopter, a ruse Banks recalled vividly. 'It was a pure publicity thing,' he recalled.

'Dick and I were having a drink one night and talking about doing something impressive and completely unrelated to what the old board might have done. If I can recall at that point, we saw a shot of a helicopter landing on top of a building and that looked pretty good. He said he knew somebody that had a chopper and "bingo"!'

Banks added: 'Actually it was a massive beast of an old bucket, looked like one of those things the Russians were using in Afghanistan and the noise inside was incredible, even with headphones on. I was thinking what happened if this thing crashed on the pitch, or even worse, just conked out and the game was cancelled? Anyway it turned out OK and it was a major bit of publicity for us, but the pilot got into a load of bother because he didn't file his flight plan correctly. I don't think I will ever go in another helicopter!'

Times were certainly changing at Northampton. The only choppers in the Cobblers' history locker had previously been the rugged defender playing type patented by Tom Smalley in the 1940s and 1950s, who simply brought down wingers as soon as look at them. Whatever next? Well, the new era also brought the video age – a match service fronted by 1970s striker Gary Mabee, who had scored thirteen league goals in 1974-75, before injury stalled his career.

Mabee recalled: 'My own highlights as a player were scoring two goals at home to Swansea either side of half-time in a 5-1 win – the second a 30-yard volley after Paul Stratford flicked on an Alan Starling goal-kick – and getting a pair at Cambridge when we came from 1-3 down at half-time to win 4-3, with Bill Dodgin running on the pitch at the end and launching himself upon me to celebrate.'

Mabee's other brace that season was also memorable in Northampton Town folklore, as he scored twice at Rotherham in a 3-1 win on a Sunday in early October. That was Phil Neal's last game for Northampton before signing for Liverpool for £60,000, a record sale for the club until they sold George Reilly to Cambridge in November 1979 for £165,000, a figure subsequently surpassed by the sale of Hill. Yet Neal played most of the Rotherham match in goal after Alan Starling's early injury, Mabee recalling: 'I remember Phil coming into the dressing room the next day looking as white as a ghost as he had just discovered Liverpool had bid for him.'

Mabee's return to the front line this time involved a video camera, in the dawn of a new technological age. Even here, boss Carr was central to the plot as he explained: 'Initially I was working close to the dugouts where Graham sat. It was really him who put me on the road as far as Anglia Television was concerned. He was always keen on having the ex-players around and fronted my cause.'

Although sceptics were disparaging of facilities at the County Ground during those days, it is worth remembering the often afflicted venue actually boasted its own royal box. Mabee explained: 'We started the match videos with the Peterborough league game in September and initially we were based on the cricket side. I remember doing the Hereford game from there, as they had Wayne Cegielski playing for them, who had been with me at Tottenham. However, we quickly moved the operation to the Meccano Stand. At the time I was a painter and decorator and did some work at RAF Brize Norton in Oxfordshire. As it was used as a base for so many royal trips abroad, they had a royal quarters where they congregated before taking off. When that was refitted, I took a lot of the panelling and doors to construct our box in the Meccano Stand.'

Mabee, fellow cameramen Barry Scriven and Tim Franks, along with commentator Richard Jordan, accessed their new vantage point by steps and began a service which has stood the test of time. Mabee added: 'Even in relegation seasons we have always compiled an end of season video, for which there are always a few takers.

'My own favourite goal from the Championship season was the Hill goal against Preston. It just summed the whole season up really – the way he just ran from halfway through the opposition's defence, destroying them with his pace, before a cool finish.

'I also interviewed Preston's manager John McGrath, which was nice for me as he had kicked me all over the park one day playing for Southampton reserves when I was at Tottenham.'

The Peterborough cup-tie was another one of those old-boy reunions, as ex-Cobblers Gage, Christie and Steve Phillips were in a Posh line-up run on a temporary stand-in basis by Lil Fuccillo, as John Wile had gone, and it would be another three days before Noel Cantwell was appointed for his second spell in charge at London Road.

Ever a character who could mix it with the best, barrel-chested Phillips had been a goalscoring favourite during his County Ground playing days and was always someone to react. He remarked: 'I've got used to taking the stick from the crowd. I used to get a lot more when I was playing here.'

The crowd of 9,114 for the Cobblers' 3-0 win was the biggest for all the first-round ties, barring Middlesbrough's 3-0 win over Blackpool, and the atmosphere was special, Carr saying: 'I was at Bootham Crescent yesterday for York's 3-1 win over Crewe and you wouldn't have known there was a football match on.'

Posh goalkeeper Kevin Shoemake was his side's man of the match, a fact which told its own story. He recalled: 'I remember it being played in the pouring rain and my dad sitting watching in the temporary stand they had put up on the cricket side. There was one special save in particular from an Ian Benjamin overhead-kick which I pushed away for a corner.

The occasion also belatedly brought a first Cobblers' goal for Gilbert from the penalty spot, which was remarkable in itself given the midfield man's sizeable input into the terrific season. Chard was out of the penalty equation against his old club due to suspension, and Gilbert almost set the ball rolling after two minutes with a vicious left-foot curler in the second minute, only for Shoemake to tip it over.

However, Gilbert's magical moment finally arrived in the 53rd minute after Jeff Doyle had upended Morley, Gilbert lashing a no-nonsense penalty high and wide of the goalkeeper's left hand. By then, McGoldrick had opened the scoring in style at the end of a sweet first-half move, while Benjamin rounded matters off thirteen minutes from time. Gilbert would go on and convert all nine of his Northampton penalties that season to make the task his own.

The twelve-day break before the next game was caused by another 'cry-off' – this time Exeter were unable to fulfil their visit at the scheduled time due to a bout of food poisoning. I would like to say the trip to Crewe on 28 November was one of those memorable highlights of the season – which of course it was – except for the fact I never actually saw the game. Instead, I spent a frustrating three hours on the M1 stuck between Junction 15 and Watford Gap Services, a hold-up caused by a tanker spilling oil. Eventually, I crawled off the motorway at 7.20pm where an emergency phone call to the home of deputy sports editor Brian Barron initiated 'Plan B' to arrange alternative copy for the Saturday paper.

Of course, it was in the days before mobile phones and even before full coverage from the local BBC radio station. As a football reporter used to conveying the news, I can't begin to describe the mortifying experience of meeting the security officer back at the *Chronicle & Echo* approximately 45 minutes later to be told the Cobblers had scored three times in the first half-hour. Hang on, who's the reporter here? Why couldn't the Cobblers have just had a night off, for goodness sake?

Hill's hat-trick that night was the last of the four he would score for the Cobblers (Preston, Torquay and Halifax the earlier ones) while also striking six doubles, all in the 1986-87 season.

The relationship between Carr and Hill was often a fiery one, the head-on clash of two strong-minded individuals which collectively could whip up into a storm, a shouting match which took time to abate. Yet once the outbursts had calmed, neither bore grudges. The evidence of all this was clear early on as their paths crossed following Hill's release by Leicester as a raw nineteen-year-old after he had been at Filbert Street for three years on an apprenticeship.

Hill recalled those early days: 'Graham was big mates with Dave Richardson, who had been my youth-team coach at Leicester and a lot of the old City reserves who had been released such as Paul Culpin and Stewart Hamill went on to Nuneaton, so it was the natural thing to do. I was sub for the first game but as I was a young lad I couldn't understand why a Leicester City reserve shouldn't be in the team at Nuneaton. When I still didn't start in the next game I had a row and stormed off.'

Carr recalled: 'I remember Hilly first turning up at Nuneaton in a blue Morris 1000, jumping out and slamming the car door. He was a bit headstrong and I got rid of him after three games!'

Shortly after, Hill read in the local *Nuneaton Tribune* that Carr was short of players, and rang him up, offering his services for the weekend, having in the meantime signed for the old Leicester City player Graham Cross at Hinckley Athletic.

'They were in a different league so it didn't matter, and I ended up playing for Nuneaton on the Saturday at centre-half in a match at Worcester which we won 1-0,' Hill said. 'I remember Graham coming onto the pitch at the end and throwing his arms around me and telling me: "you are staying here!" I had made a point and our relationship grew from that point and we had a mutual respect. Let's face it, apart from my father Keith, Graham was always my mentor in football.'

Not that the tantrums ended there, by any means, the severity of the Cobblers' training being one of the major triggers for strain, both on the pre-season tours of the north-east for which Carr became famous for organising, and back home on the hillier section climbs of the Northampton parks, the Racecourse and Abington Park.

Hill said: 'On the tours we would play matches at places like Frickley on the Saturday, Gretna Green on the Sunday, and Blue Star on the Monday night after training early every morning on the sand dunes by the sea. I remember it came to a Tuesday night where we were beaten 0-2 at Blyth Spartans, or somewhere like that, and Graham went mad. So did I, as I told him in the dressing room in no uncertain terms that we were absolutely "cream-crackered" and I wasn't playing the next night.'

The pair slept on the fall-out and Hill recalls bumping into his manager first thing the next morning in the corridor before breakfast, where it was all back to normal. 'He was the last person I wanted to see at that moment but he just said "Morning Hilly, are you alright?" It was as though nothing had happened.' Yet it clearly had, as Hill sat in the stands and missed that night's friendly, much to the envy of his team-mates.

The policy of persecution training from 7am on the sands continued for several seasons to come, the Cobblers' true abilities disguised by many of their pre-season results which were often lost to inferior opposition as they were simply whacked out by the intensity of the schedules.

Mind you, skipper Morley once recalled leaving an Indian restaurant at around 2.30 in the morning full of curry and beer, with characters such as McGoldrick and Reed in tow. They were still out running after just three hours sleep, understandably not in the best shape. Morley said: 'I had never felt so ill in my life. Mind you, ever since then I've never set a lot of store by pre-season results. Sometimes I think it can be a good thing to lose them as it helps to iron out your problems. I remember us once going down 1-4 to a lesser team when we were all over the place.'

A notable example of this was the opening day of the 1987-88 season when pre-season concerns surrounding the team's results were blown out of the water by a 5-0 victory at Chester. On balance, you'd probably have settled for that.

Back at home, Hill recalled the Increase & Demand training strategy devised by Carr and put in place by coach Walker and physio Casey. On a football pitch split into six sectors, including each of the corners and two halfway points, it meant starting off by sprinting the first short leg, before trotting the remainder, then sprinting two, three, four, five and all six, scaling down the gentler trotting each time, before either repeating the process or winding it down.

On other occasions the players would be split into four groups, run four laps and rest, complete 2x800m and rest, 4x400m, 6x200, 6x100m and 6x50m. It physically brought them to the end of their tether.

Even that didn't fully satisfy Carr in his desire to make his team of talented footballers ultra-fit. He swapped the site to the pitches at the

Leicester Street end of the town's Racecourse so it could all take place on a gradient. Spiked shoes were used for a similar process on the athletics track at the town's British Timken sports ground, Hill admitting: 'I was OK at the sprints but rubbish at the long distance stuff – people like Eddie McGoldrick and Phil Chard were good at those. There was a time when a lot of the players didn't sleep on a Sunday night because they knew what was coming on a Monday with the runs and I was physically sick on a few occasions. There was a point high up on Abington Park near the golf course where we used to have a rest behind a hedge and then come out again after our breather!'

Ultimately though, the Carr strategy worked, earning the respect of the players. 'You have to say it paid off and we became an even better team for it as we won the league title,' said Hill, who also reinforced the point about discarded players anxious to grab the olive branch extended them.

'Perhaps other players wouldn't have taken those Monday morning runs at Abington Park and I believe later on that quite a few didn't,' he said.

'As a team, we were nearly all on second, third or even fourth chances. Virtually all of the players had been turned away somewhere else – myself at Leicester, Trevor at Derby, Peter Gleasure (Millwall), Graham Reed (Barnsley), Russ Wilcox (Doncaster and Cambridge), Keith McPherson and Warren Donald (West Ham), Dave Gilbert (Lincoln), Ian Benjamin (West Brom), and even Phil Chard and Eddie McGoldrick to an extent. We all wanted success badly. Graham wanted people around him who shared his values and ambition. He was desperate to succeed and could never understand why someone would want to play football without the strong desire of winning the league. Sure, I had my stand-up rows with him but he never bore a grudge.'

It was natural Carr should have wanted to bring Hill and Morley to Northampton, and Hill scored 23 goals in the 23 league games between 17 September and 6 February, netting in all but seven. It was this phase of the campaign which so glaringly highlighted his development into a midfield player, albeit an unorthodox one with an electric burst of pace over short distances which frequently left defenders trailing in his wake.

Despite his outgoing and reactionary nature, he was willing to learn, and Benjamin for one recalled: 'Richard came to me at the end of the 1985-86 season and wanted help on his finishing. I said: "You're joking, aren't you? You've just scored nineteen goals." Yet he was concerned he had missed so many chances, so I told him to try passing the ball rather than blasting it into the net and I think he took that on board.'

When the Exeter game did take place on the following Tuesday evening, the Cobblers became the first team in the country to score 50 league goals that season, and what's more they did it against a side who had easily the country's best defensive league record at the time – losing only two of their first seventeen matches and conceding only eleven goals in the process. Curiously, for all their proficiency at keeping goals out, Exeter failed to win away from home all that season, drawing thirteen of their 23 Today League games.

Well, to put it quite simply, the Cobblers led 3-0 after 38 minutes and it was game, set and match, Morley, McGoldrick and Hill making it onto the scoresheet.

Thrilling Friday nights out in Essex at Southend might not sound everybody's cup of tea, but after the 4-0 win in 1985-86, Cobblers fans were becoming acclimatised to the idea and the evening of 5 December would scale fresh heights. With the second round FA Cup tie level at 4-4 with 24 minutes to go, there was always a chance the press-box abacus would run out of beads. However, it stopped there.

With Morley sidelined thanks to a poisoned ankle, the Cobblers were missing their inspirational skipper but at least Donald and Chard returned after suspension. Quick goals early on by Donald and Southend's Richard Cadette hardly prepared the crowd for what was to follow in the early second-half salvo. Cadette (2-1 to the home side), Hill (2-2), Hill again (2-3), Cadette (3-3), Benjamin (3-4) and finally Roy McDonough (4-4). So excited was I that, almost two hours later, I almost missed the slip road exit for the A12 turn-off and briefly drove onto the embankment. At least one Cobblers season-ticket holder has never let me forget that moment and only now allows me to drive him as far as Holcot.

By the time the replay came round five days later all and sundry knew the reward was a trip to Newcastle United. This would have been thrilling enough, but as the Magpies were struggling and it would mean a nostalgic return to the north-east for boss Carr, everyone was practically beside themselves with anticipation. Perhaps the players also thought it meant they wouldn't get a north-east tour before the following season. One logical assumption might have been that the manager would already have completed his round of visiting the relatives.

Early celebrations were muted, as Glenn Pennyfather put the Shrimpers ahead after six minutes, although Benjamin's equaliser, a few hours before he could start celebrating his 26th birthday in earnest, helped calm the nerves. Yet Cadette's goal to make it 2-1 before the break, a score which remained heading into the tie's final quarter, suggested all was not well.

It was at this point that the half-time replacement of referee Ray Lewis by senior linesman John Penn assumed greater significance, with the Great Bookham official forced to step down with a pulled hamstring. The Cobblers won the tie with two Gilbert penalties inside the space of seven minutes. After 74 minutes skipper Morley was brought down by future Cobbler Danny O'Shea, Gilbert sending Jim Stannard the wrong way with a spot-kick directed to his right. Penn then turned down an appeal for an apparent foul on Benjamin before again pointing to the spot with ten minutes left after McGoldrick was fouled by Paul Roberts.

If Southend had questioned the air of County Ground invincibility, then Wrexham took the process a stage further three days later by daring to become the first visiting side to seize a point there during 1986-87 after nine straight home wins. Perhaps it was simply the aftermath of the Southend frenzy, although the Red Dragons had their own cup distractions during this campaign, notably in Europe, where they claimed the scalp of FC Zurreiq from Malta in the European Cup-Winners' Cup 7-0 on aggregate, before going out to Real Zaragoza on the away-goals rule at the second hurdle in early November.

Nationally, eleven players were sent off across the country, four of them at Sheffield United, where three of the visiting Portsmouth players took an early bath during a 0-1 defeat. The Cobblers' chief concern was the fact it was the first occasion all season they failed to score in the first half of a league match as they trailed 0-1. Jim Steele restored Wrexham's lead after Wilcox's first goal for the club, but Benjamin spared blushes.

It would also be negligent not to mention a pre-match presentation made to Harry Warden before the Wrexham game by Brian Walden and Les Underwood of the Northants Football Association. Warden was a remarkable character and servant around the County Ground who put true meaning into the phrase 'multi-tasking' long before it ever came into common usage.

Prior to the season opener with Torquay, Warden had been presented with a carriage clock by vice-president Stuart Wilson after retiring at the age of 91 at the end of the 1985-86 season. Since his involvement with the club had gone back to 1921, the connection with a timepiece was a fitting one as it meant he had completed 65 years of service.

Quite simply, Warden was Northampton through and though, having worked for the town's Church's shoe company for many years and lived close to the town centre off Clare Street. It appeared Warden had a fascination for claret paint during the summer months when the County Ground was receiving its annual dose of restorative treatment. 'If you stood still long enough, chances are you would be painted claret,' said one of his willing former helpers. The onerous summer task of hacking back the weeds behind the Spion Kop also required attention to detail. 'Harry was insistent we didn't dig out the ferns.'

Warden had something of a love-hate relationship with cricket club secretary Ken Turner, perhaps not surprising given the uncomfortable overlap with the Northants CCC outfield and Northampton Town's right wing, if you were attacking the Spion Kop end. 'He was a lovely man, but woe betide any cricket supporters who parked in the roped off goal-mouth areas during the summer months,' recalled his devoted one-time odd-job man and turnstile operator. 'He was also a good mathematician who knew all about the gate receipts and worked very closely with Dave Bowen for years.'

Wrexham's sixteen-match unbeaten run ended the following Friday with a 1-2 loss at Stockport, while Lincoln's impressive form in the run up to their 21 December visit, a 4-0 win over Swansea, counted for nothing as they went down 1-3 at the County Ground.

In between, the Cobblers had the novelty of actually losing a match, but their opening 0-1 Freight Rover Trophy loss at Gillingham, a repeat of their first leg Littlewoods Cup result, was hardly of earth tremor stuff and didn't prevent them progressing through the group stages.

The Imps hadn't conceded a goal in winning three of their previous four matches and took the lead midway through the first half through Gary Lund, a hat-trick hero against the Swans. Yet Gilbert squared matters up from the spot just before the break after Hill was brought down by Gary West. McGoldrick headed the Cobblers in front nine minutes after the restart, although Benjamin's strike, a real peach after he turned and nutmegged a defender on the by-line before curling an exquisite shot from a tight angle into the far corner past goalkeeper Swinburne, was one of the highlights of the season and a trick he would repeat at Peterborough a month later.

Christmas was coming, the drums were starting to roll for a pantomime season, but what the Cobblers had lying in store would have exceeded most supporters' expectations, even in a season which had drawn breath on an even more disbelieving scale from a Northampton public not used to being fed from this sumptuous banquet table.

In the *Chronicle & Echo* I had a bizarre stab at scripting a Cobblers' Christmas spectacular production, which featured chairman Banks as Aladdin, manager Carr the GGG (Genial Geordie Genie) while other key roles in a hybrid production included: Morley (Prince Charming), Hill (Cowardly Lion), McPherson (Dick Whittington), Gilbert (Puss-In-Football Boots), McGoldrick (Jack) The Beanstalk (Wakeley Gage), and even a Fiery Red Dragon role incorporating Dixie McNeil and Terry Yorath due to the management roles they were carrying out at Wrexham and Swansea. Not wishing to be omitted from a huge cast of characters, I managed to somehow cast myself as Dorothy, with sidekick snapper Norton as Toto. It might not have been *The Yellow Brick Road* but the A127 to Southend certainly assumed dream-like qualities.

It wouldn't just have been negative 'Northampton mentality' to suggest that greater expectations were unrealistic. Let's face it, the past three visits had brought a 4-0 league win in 1985-86, a 3-1 success there in the Freight Rover Trophy in March, and then the 4-4 FA Cup thriller.

Yet the seasonal recipe seemed to suggest that a trip to Southend's Roots Hall in December meant the Cobblers scoring four goals. Even bringing the kick-off forward to 11.30am wasn't going to change that, although High Noon would have been more appropriate as a showdown between the division's top two clubs.

For me, it was the one occasion during the season (apart from the return journey from Newcastle the following month) when I travelled on the team coach. I still have vivid memories of walking into the County Ground players' entrance around 4pm on Christmas Day – barely time to digest the Queen's Speech before witnessing the players' last circuit of the pitch before they changed and boarded the team bus to Essex. It seemed to sum up the sure professionalism of the approach. Perhaps there had been the odd sliver of turkey but all the odd jokes about excessive Christmas pudding would surely have come back to haunt them as they circuited the Football League's longest pitch.

The journey to the hotel at Hornchurch was uneventful enough – I don't think any over-enthusiastic but short-sighted Essex football supporters asked me for an autograph as I disembarked. In fact the chief recollection was sitting round the bar with Messrs Walker, Carr and Casey having a Christmas drink, after the players had been packed off to bed. Later in the season when I interviewed Morley he summed it up by saying this would be remembered as 'the season when the Cobblers went unbeaten for six months in the league and Clive Walker finally bought a round of drinks'. While the coach's reputation for deep pockets might be true, I was the one who didn't delve into my wallet on that occasion and the fact has preyed on my conscience for 25 years.

After the drama of the Cobblers' FA Cup-ties, the Shrimpers had continued in the same vein by beating Cambridge 5-4 in the Associate Members Trophy, but then perversely drawing 0-0 with Stockport County, which would have been a tough one to predict, before winning at Wolves.

Two sent off, eight booked by referee Alf Buksh, but the dismissals of McDonough for Southend and Gilbert for the Cobblers were bit-part incidents in an overall picture which saw Carr's troops stretch their lead at the top to seventeen points, averaging almost three goals a game at this juncture.

Curiously, the goalscorers were identical to those in the FA Cup thriller, Hill (two), Benjamin and Donald hitting the target. In the *Chronicle & Echo*, I wrote: 'The second half goals from Hill and Donald were the finest Christmas fare you could hope for, both pearls in a season littered with memorable strikes.'

Despite this, the Cobblers failed to manage a goal-attempt for the first half-hour, only to seize the initiative with Hill's header from a Chard cross, after the first effort with his foot had merely bobbled upwards under a Southend challenge. Another right-wing break, this time by Mann, in for flu victim McGoldrick, brought the second, when Stannard was unable to hold the stinging low cross from the by-line, allowing Benjamin to lash home his fifteenth goal of the season.

The master-class strikes derived from Morley robbing O'Shea with twenty minutes left, allowing him to cut inside and feed Hill, who scored with a terrific left-footer, before Donald unleashed an astonishing 40-yard strike after approach play by Gilbert, Gernon and Benjamin.

In the meantime McDonough had been sent off for a foul on McPherson, while Gilbert joined him in the final minute after appearing to kick out at Cadette.

You can't begin to appreciate the 'job done' feeling of satisfaction, riding home on the coach on what I remember to be a bright, crisp December afternoon (I might just have imagined the blue-sky thinking) while other scores in the afternoon kick-offs filtered in. It really was another age – in Division One, Norwich 2 Nottingham For 1 (Norwich went fourth 24 hours later after winning 1-0 at Manchester United), Liverpool 1 Manchester United 0, Luton 0 Watford 2, Newcastle 0 Everton 4, to name but a few.

The Cobblers' next opponents, on 28 December, were Cardiff, who had held Swansea 0-0 at Boxing Day. In fact the Cobblers' own success was put in context by the fact that seven of Division Four's Boxing Day matches ended in draws, notably Crewe's 2-2 effort with Preston. Bizarrely, Hereford were the only home winners with a 2-0 success over Wolves. The Cobblers were still stretching their advantage at the top.

A packed County Ground groaned fit to bursting under the strain of a crowd of 11,138, the best league gate for thirteen seasons, when a 0-1 home defeat by Peterborough was watched by 11,378. The kick-off was delayed by ten minutes, and there were even comparisons to be drawn with the Boxing Day match against Chelsea in Division One in 1965, when an entrance gate was charged down and officially 23,325 witnessed a 2-3 defeat.

Cardiff were enduring their first ever season in Division Four but had still knocked Chelsea out of the Littlewoods Cup and should have been no pushovers. However, Benjamin put the Cobblers ahead inside four minutes after being sent clear by Gilbert, his shot going in off a post.

Cardiff equalised through Chris Pike, only to have keeper Graham Moseley dismissed five minutes later. He had hauled down Hill outside the box as he chased a Morley flick-on, referee Malcolm Cotton being left in no doubts.

The Cobblers were back in front before the changearound after Chris Marustik hacked down McGoldrick, allowing Gilbert to tuck away the penalty and beat stand-in goalkeeper Michael Ford. The second half brought further goals by Morley and Hill before Carr's men took their foot off the pedal.

While the dawn of a New Year invariably brings thoughts of change, surely few people could have expected the rarity of a goalless first half when the Cobblers tackled Colchester, who had lost three of their four league matches in December to slip to eighth place.

The visitors had the best chances in a low-key first period but this was only a prelude to four goals in sixteen minutes after the restart. The Cobblers twice led through Benjamin and Morley, only for Colchester to hit back on each occasion via Tony Adcock, later to become a Cobblers player.

The points were decided five minutes from time when a handball incident saw referee Danny Vickers point to the spot after Hill's pace onto a back-pass had created the drama. Goalkeeper Alec Chamberlain got both hands to Gilbert's penalty, but the ball bounced up into the net.

Gernon played his last game on loan before returning to Ipswich in the 1-1 draw at Exeter 48 hours later, as Saturday football briefly returned before the disruption of the English winter kicked in, although the pools panel did sit for the first of five occasions on that afternoon.

Exeter's durability under Colin Appleton was such that they had not lost a league game until 1 November, going down to a late goal at Preston, and the same opponents also inflicted their first home defeat in early March.

Far more interesting events unfolded the next day when boss Carr received a message from his wife Chris to ring back Oxford United chairman Robert Maxwell, the late media-magnate. Was this a spoof? Not at bit of it. When Carr did so, the question was a simple one: 'How much for the boy Hill?'

The 'boy Hill' had just struck his 26th goal of the season to ensure that the Cobblers equalled a club record of scoring in 24 straight league games. Such exploits could not go unnoticed, especially as Oxford were planning to replace Liverpool-bound John Aldridge, who moved to Merseyside for £750,000 at the end of that month. The Cobblers found themselves in a chain which even linked to Ian Rush's move to Juventus.

However, Carr's answer was a snub to the printing tycoon: 'A lot of other clubs have shown interest and we are not interested in doing anything until the summer,' he reported, having almost in his previous breath knocked back a 'derisory' £30,000 bid from Coventry for Chard. The Cobblers' exploits were prompting twitching in board rooms across the country on an ever-increasing scale.

One player still anxious to carve out his name in the professional ranks was Northampton lad Aidy Mann, who grabbed an opportunity to shine in the 3-0 Freight Rover Trophy win over Notts County on the Monday evening.

Since County had already lost 0-5 at home to Gillingham in their other Group Six round-robin match, it could be argued the Division Three side weren't committed to this cause, but Cobblers goals by Hill, Gilbert and Mann provided an excellent morale-boost in what should have been the final preparation for the Newcastle FA Cup-tie five days away.

Technically, it was the final warm-up although, as it turned out, the tie was still sixteen days away.

CHAPTER SIX

Newcastle – A Bridge Too Far

Close examination of the playing career of Trevor William Morley provides more evidence that miracles certainly can, and do happen. Proceeding logically with this thread, if you make this man your captain, the remarkable 1986-87 season fashioned by Northampton Town becomes almost a natural chain of events.

Manager Carr not only took Morley from Corby to Nuneaton, he also made him Priority No 1 when assembling the Cobblers' task force. Not only that, he installed him as captain. 'It would have broken my heart if I hadn't been allowed to sign him,' he confessed.

Why shouldn't he have been allowed to recruit the Nottingham-born player who had been told as a teenager at Derby that he simply wasn't good enough after a two-year apprenticeship at the Baseball Ground? After all, the player, like the bulk of his new County Ground team-mates, was desperate to grab the second chance at a football career.

He also looked like a skipper, standing out from the crowd with his swarthy, striking appearance and long, curly dark hair. At one stage he could have been mistaken as a forerunner of Johnny Depp as Captain Jack Sparrow starring in *Pirates of the Caribbean*. I could also easily imagine him as a Royalist commander alongside Prince Rupert at the Battle of Naseby, especially as he lived for a while in the village of Brixworth just five miles up the road from this historic 1645 site from the English Civil War. That was until it dawned on me that the Royalists lost, which didn't make any sense at all. Put another way, and the visual impression of Morley, McGoldrick and Hill wasn't far removed from a remake of *The Three Musketeers*, with perhaps even Wilcox thrown in as D'Artagnan. Better than *Goldilocks and the Three Bears* anyway.

Apart from being rescued by Carr from the football scrapheap, the miracle part of the Morley story, and the reason for doubt over his signature, stemmed from a series of career injuries which would have finished a lesser man. He had an extraordinary right knee. Throughout his career, it was always vulnerable as well as being an odd shape. Problems surrounding it surfaced at regular intervals during his career and did so again in the third round Newcastle FA Cup-tie, finally played on 21 January after four postponements.

It is no coincidence that Morley's subsequent six-week injury absence brought the most languid phase of an otherwise memorable campaign.

Perhaps it worth remembering that sometimes in life we have to endure a little of the banal, to fully appreciate the boon-time.

Consider it like this. Starting with the 5-0 hammering of Crewe in November, the Cobblers played twelve matches in an action-packed 38 days but the action levels subsided somewhat after 5 January, with just six fixtures spread across the next 40 days

Only one of that first frenetic schedule of matches was lost – the relatively meaningless Freight Rover Trophy tie at Gillingham – so three reverses in the more leisurely phase that followed represented something of a dip in achievement levels, though on closer analysis the defeats were hardly critical in the overall objective of achieving promotion to Division Three.

When initially approached by Corby Town, Morley was a midfield player, but The Steelmen needed a striker. His adaptability proved a success. Six months down the line he was spotted and signed by Carr for Nuneaton for £11,000 in a deal that also involved Derek Walker.

During three and a half largely successful seasons at Manor Park with Carr, Morley won six international caps at semi-professional level but was sidelined after a horrendous injury in a match at Milton Keynes. He explained: 'I landed on the side of my leg. When I looked at it, I saw the leg was straight but the knee was sticking out in a different direction. I had to push it back in.'

Apart from prompting any initial feeling of nausea, such a basic weakness raised question marks over whether he would ever play football again, let alone aspire to professional level. He said: 'It meant six months wearing a giant plaster cast all the way from the top of my thigh, right down to my ankle. I was working on a fruit and vegetable market in Derby at the time and needed to drive a lorry to work for deliveries. I couldn't sit up, so I was standing and driving in the seat all the time. Somehow I managed to do it.'

Remarkably, Morley's attention to fitness routine meant he was not a lost cause and evidence of the 'dodgy knee' could be filed in a dusty cabinet once more, although it would resurface and his relationship with physiotherapist Casey became closer as a result, not least as they were living just a couple of miles apart.

When Morley sustained a poisoned ankle during 1986-87, Casey recalled: 'I had a phone call from Trevor at around midnight, asking if he could have anti-inflammatory tablets and pain-killers. I went right out to his house and gave him the medication. The ankle had swollen to twice the size as normal. There appeared no way on the Thursday morning he would be able to play on the Saturday, but Trevor's attitude to work was always amazing. I have never known a player to work so hard. We strapped him up and you wouldn't have known anything was wrong.'

He added: 'After the game it blew up again and we packed it in ice. There was a game on the Tuesday and again he played with strapping.' It is not unusual for players in winning teams to insist on turning out, but Morley took this trend to new dimensions.

As if the recurring knee and the ankle poisoning were not enough throughout his Cobblers career, Morley also overcame the acute pelvic strain leading into his groin which was thought to need an operation before the 1986-87 season kicked off at Scunthorpe. Much later on in his career he arguably capped that by having a steel plate in his head after fracturing his skull while playing for Reading at Portsmouth during the 1995-96 season.

Perversely, the saga of the pelvic strain also included a pivotal miracle moment, and the sort of lucky twist Morley was always anxious to avoid with his knee. After initially consulting a Harley Street specialist, the captain was minutes away from surgery being carried out in Northampton. It had even reached the stage where he had even taken his 'pre-medical' tablet, when the London doctor rang to say he had reconsidered.

Instead, Casey and Morley intensified exercises and miraculously, the player started the campaign to the surprise of all. Who knows what the consequences might have been had the operation gone ahead.

Carr's determination to make sure there were no hitches in signing Morley for the Cobblers knew no bounds. As well as impressing on Morley the need to persuade Cobblers' club doctor Joseph Ciappara that he had never suffered any serious knee problems, he also told him to knock a year off his age when his signature was required.

'I was 23 at the time, but Graham suggested I say I was only 22 as he thought that sounded a bit old,' said Morley. This was something which then followed me through my career and could have been a problem, if for instance, someone had ever taken me to court.' For the record, Morley was born on 20 March 1961.

The responsibility placed on the skipper's relatively young shoulders was substantial but was milked as a positive feed. He said: 'Graham Carr and I always had a good relationship and he was like a father to me. He was the most important figure in my career, taught me great lessons and had a giant personality. He gave me a lot of influence. Taking me to Northampton and making me his captain meant I had a lot of confidence. He always brought the team together after a game and people could sort out their problems. The atmosphere was absolutely fantastic and Graham was a big part of that. I am not saying it is good for footballers to go out and drink lots of alcohol, but I still believe that bonding is something they have lost somewhere in the modern game.'

Living in Norway for twelve years, Morley sorely missed the English pub culture and the social element that went with it – a large factor in him pining for a return home with his second wife Samira. There was no shortage of that under Carr, as Morley said: 'The dressing room spirit at Northampton was almost unreal. We knew we were going to win matches. There was a lot of psychology going on. One example came when we used to make tea for the opposition. Clive Walker would taste it and say something like: "that's too good for them," and pour some cold water in.' Morley recalled how Carr would lie almost on the floor against the door in the home dressing room to hear what was going on next door in a barely covert spying mission.

Hill, meanwhile, was a leading activist when it came to banging on the visitors' door and shouting as the team filed past: 'It was like a fortress playing at home, as though we were invincible,' recalled Morley. 'In a way it wasn't dissimilar to Nuneaton as we went two years without being beaten at home there.' The Cobblers had become kings of their castle. They even viewed the Newcastle tie as a winnable game on their travels, although the delay in playing it didn't assist their cause and Morley admitted there was almost a sense of feeling cheated as events unfolded.

He said: 'We genuinely felt we had a great chance of beating Newcastle, as it didn't look like Peter Beardsley would play due to injury when the tie was first scheduled. Let's face it, at Northampton we had so many good players around us. Almost all of the credit for that came down to Graham Carr. When you look at it, he didn't make many mistakes.'

Wherever you turned, it seemed, there were players ticking the correct boxes. No square pegs in round holes here, as Morley added: 'We had players such as Dave Gilbert, Eddie McGoldrick and Warren Donald around. Graham Reed was my best mate and although he was never the greatest footballer, Graham knew how to get the best from him.'

Morley added: 'Even though I went on to play at a higher level in football, I still look back on my time at Northampton with incredible fondness and among the best days of my career.'

The strong affinity between manager and certain players meant Carr recalled driving to Manchester City with club vice-chairman Dick Underwood to watch Morley's Division Two debut against Aston Villa in January 1988 and saying: 'We were kicking every ball for him that day.' City lost that game 0-2 but Villa were promoted back to Division One that season, behind champions Millwall, so it was a testing baptism.

At Maine Road, Morley scored twelve goals in fifteen games as City won promotion back to Division One the following season, runners-up to Chelsea, who had come down the previous year after losing in the play-offs to Middlesbrough.

Returning to the top flight, City fans happily recall a 5-1 local derby win over Manchester United at Maine Road in September 1989, as they had won only one of their first six games back among the elite and the experience proved a total release. 'The United fans were singing "Fergie out" but the City fans sang "Fergie in",' recalled Morley. 'I scored one of the goals and it was a fantastic day.' Years later, City supporters still dredge up a 'Morley, Morley' chant. The legend it seems lives on.

Mel Machin's replacement by Howard Kendall at Maine Road was a catalyst which helped switch Morley and his best pal Ian Bishop to West Ham at the end of 1989, in a deal which saw Mark Ward move in the opposite direction.

Morley's 178 appearances and 57 goals for the Hammers proved both his most productive and endearing attachment, as he was player of the year in 1993-94 and also top scorer on three occasions, with thirteen goals in that season, having bagged twelve to top the charts in 1990-91 and twenty in 1992-93. A stand-out occasion was a 4-1 win at Spurs in 1994, in which he scored twice. 'It was a day which meant a lot to me for many reasons as Tottenham had tried to sign me and my mum and step-dad were there as well,' he said.

Morley's father Bill had also been a professional footballer, a 'play anywhere' forward for Nottingham Forest, who had joined them in August 1945 after joining from Mapperley Celtic. He later reverted to being a strong tackling defender and was in the Forest team which won the Division Three (South) Championship in 1951, and was still there when that side won promotion to Division One six years later.

Morley's own talents made him a natural talismanic leader, and teammate Benjamin admitted to being in awe of him the first time they played together, saying: 'It was in a pre-season friendly at Notts County and the game just passed me by. I just kept thinking how good a player Trevor was, and asking myself how he could have been hidden away in the non-league for so long.' Benjamin added: 'It took me a few games to really sort out how I was going to play with him. Trevor wanted to take so much on himself all the while. I think that was one of the reasons why early on, he didn't score any bulk of goals himself. He was so involved in everything else going on.'

That habit of taking responsibility was something which has manifested itself in other walks of the Morley life. In his early days at the

Cobblers he recalled living in digs near the Racecourse and cooking meals for some of the club apprentices who also lodged there. In Norway, his business edge became hardened by renting out three large shelter houses and 50 or so rooms, working with the local council and in many cases offering a roof to drug addicts and the under-privileged: 'It is hard work and you are always on call but I get a good sense of satisfaction in helping these people and they have a respect for me. A lot of them are good and kind people who have had bad experiences although we have had one murder and there are frequently problems arising.'

A dabble around the lower leagues in football management in Norway and work as a television soccer pundit for TV2 (a Norwegian television station) has kept him closely in touch with the game.

Benjamin may indeed have been named the club's Player of the Year for 1986-87 but he explained: 'Trevor should have won it that season, although to be honest my favourite player was Dave Gilbert. It was the way he used to wriggle with the ball and he had such a lovely left foot. He used to mesmerise people with his feet.'

Bizarrely, despite scoring 49 goals between them that season, neither Hill nor Morley made the first three in the players' award poll in the *Chronicle & Echo*, ever-present McPherson and the impish Gilbert the other men in the frame.

Gilbert was forced to miss the Newcastle FA Cup-tie through suspension, following his dismissal at Southend, even though the ice-stricken third-round clash would be postponed four times by Carlisle referee Colin Seel (perhaps Seal would have been more appropriate) from 10 January onwards. It finally took place on a Wednesday evening, eleven days later.

The tie was one of only four scheduled ties which didn't take place on its initial date, although nearby Middlesbrough were beaten 0-1 at home by Preston, who went out at Newcastle at the next hurdle. From a viewing aspect, boss Carr and the local press corps had to settle for a 3-1 come-from-behind success for Division One Watford against non-league Maidstone at Vicarage Road.

The continuing 'on-off' saga of the tie forced a series of wasted journeys. Chairman Banks and his directors travelled up for the first weekend, ultimately in the hope that the match would be played on the Monday evening, which of course it wasn't.

There was some irritation over Newcastle's 'efforts' to get the tie on. Chairman Banks noted: 'Newcastle knew Irvin Gernon was due to go back to Ipswich and we were flying high. They didn't even bother to put hay on the pitch or take any sort of precaution against the weather which was expected, and they annoyed a lot of people. There were one or two arguments in the boardroom after the game.'

Banks' only consolation had come a little earlier, when he attended Watford's 1-0 win over the Magpies on 27 December, the day after the Cobblers won 4-0 at Southend: 'I was in the boardroom after the game on that one occasion with Elton John and Tom Whalley who ran the Watford youth team and the scotch was flowing from a bottomless bottle. I had another dig at the Newcastle chairman who was going on about how the fans knew nothing about running a club. I told him his club was going nowhere until they got rid of all the old farts and put in people who matched the passion of the fans and the potential of the club – needless to say he left very quickly and we all got blind drunk, but happy!'

Coaches and trains, the latter appropriately enough via Peterborough, were planned and cancelled. It was estimated that the Cobblers' ultimate following to St James' Park was vastly reduced from what would have been 5,000 waving claret and white scarves, to around 2,000 finally making the trip.

The inclement weather put a temporary stall on everything, the next Saturday's trip to Torquay also going by the board. Optimistically believing the Magpies clash would go ahead on Monday, 19 January, the side travelled up to the north-east on the Saturday, expecting to see Newcastle's match with Spurs by way of an acclimatisation to the atmosphere – only for that to also be called off.

The happy band of largely ex semi-pros were indulging in the jet-set lifestyle and McGoldrick said: 'The players thought it was fantastic at the time, as we ended up staying in the Gosforth Park Hotel for something like four nights.' The club had taken the liberal view it would be best to 'sit it out' in Newcastle until the match was eventually played, which it was two days later.

There is no doubt Newcastle were in a vulnerable position when the tie was given the green light, sitting bottom of Division One as they were. Carr had been a young terrace Newcastle fan as a boy: 'I used to watch players like Jimmy Scoular, Ivor Allchurch, Jackie Milburn and Scottish international Jack Mitchell,' he said. The Cobblers boss had even seen the Magpies humbled 1-2 at home by Bedford Town in 1964, with future Scottish international manager Jock Wallace in goal for Bedford. All those memories simply made the prospect of taking his own side back to his home town more mouth-watering and frustrating in equal measure, as it was continually delayed.

Yet finally his chance to create some history on the north-east arrived. Newcastle, under Willie McFaul, went into the fixture on the back of five consecutive defeats, their last win being a 3-2 success against Nottingham Forest on 13 December.

Beardsley, however, who had celebrated his 26th birthday on the Saturday, had by now recovered sufficiently from his knee injury, enough to turn out anyway. Perhaps his mere presence made a difference to the Geordies' spirits, even if he didn't have the expected impact. At this stage of his career he had yet to score a Cup goal for the Magpies and this sequence extended beyond at least round three.

When the Newcastle match kicked off, the Cobblers had hardly accustomed themselves to the wall of sound created by the Gallowgate roar when they fell behind in the second minute, the former West Ham striker Paul Goddard racing clear onto David McCreery's looping header, which dropped beyond the Cobblers' back line, to score. This was an unhappy moment for on-loan Chelsea defender John Millar, whose failure to connect with the Cobblers' offside trap proved disastrous.

Matters took a further turn for the worse in the 23rd minute, when Morley's tussle with Peter Jackson led to his notorious knee being sprung from its socket. Morley recalled: 'I was twisted a bit by Jackson and while my studs stayed put in the turf my knee spun round. The knee was always weak but I had my revenge against him years later when I played for Manchester City against Bradford City when he was the Bradford centre-half.' That match was the final game of the 1988-89 campaign on 13 May when Morley scored in a 1-1 draw for City at Bradford, a result which clinched the second promotion place for Mel Machin's side ahead of a Crystal Palace side which included McGoldrick, who had joined the Eagles in the January of that year.

Despite the spirited introduction of Mann at St James' Park, the Cobblers were undoubtedly weakened, yet still managed to draw level midway through the second period when Chard's cross was nodded back from the far post by McGoldrick, enabling Hill to rifle home into the corner from twelve yards.

Joy spread among the travelling band of Cobblers fans, yet cruelly it only lasted a minute as a shot by Andy Thomas, a match-winner against the Cobblers for Oxford the previous year in the Milk Cup, was blocked by Reed only to hit the hapless Millar and the ball rolled into the net for what turned out to be the winner.

Tributes to the Cobblers' effort were fulsome, including one from Tyneside giant Jackie Milburn who remarked: 'You'll obviously win Division Four and can go on and win the third as well.'

Carr himself took a phlegmatic view on the outcome and said: 'I would have been sick at the result if we had been bottom of the table and needed something to keep our season going,' while Wilcox was among many unfazed by the Division One side: 'Our style didn't suit them at all. They dropped too deep, and if you keep them outside the box, you've got a chance,' he said.

While Newcastle escaped the evening believing they had avoided an embarrassing banana-skin, on a par with Bedford in 1964, or their Hereford demise in 1972, they probably surprised a few people themselves, climbing from the foot of the Division One to finish a comparatively respectable seventeenth. After losing 0-1 at eventual beaten finalists Spurs in the fifth round of the FA Cup, the Magpies won seven of their eleven Today League matches from the beginning of March to cement their position.

Unexpected spin-offs are frequently the outcome of such high-profile contests – it's just a case of pinpointing exactly what will happen. On this occasion, the presence of Republic of Ireland manager Jack Charlton set tongues wagging that an international call might be on the horizon for McGoldrick.

A Corby lad, McGoldrick moved to the town aged one from London, after being born on the Blackstock Road, just a mile from Arsenal's ground where he later played. Yet the fact his parents Ron and Maura hailed from Dublin gave him all the legitimate family claims to a Republic of Ireland career he needed.

While the 21-year-old winger had taken time to acclimatise to the full-time game, there was no doubting his value to the trail-blazing side as the width his game offered helped stretch defences and create room for team-mates, such as Hill inside.

There was also never any doubt of his appreciating being given the chance to step up in grade. Quoted in the season's *News of the World* annual as saying simply: 'You don't know how good it is to be a professional footballer,' McGoldrick went on to maximise his potential by playing for Arsenal, Crystal Palace and Manchester City.

In fact, it would be another five years before McGoldrick made an international bow, winning fifteen full caps and one 'B' appearance. Who would have seen that coming, when Carr took him to Nuneaton from Kettering Town as a raw teenager, or indeed when vice-chairman Dick Underwood slapped his cheque-book on the roof of a car parked outside 195 Abington Avenue and wrote out a payment for £15,000 to secure the joint services of him and goalkeeper Alan Harris in 1986?

McGoldrick's international career peaked during qualification to the 1994 World Cup in the USA where, although he was part of the Ireland squad, he never played. Yet he appeared in four of the twelve qualifiers, including 90 minutes at an inflamed Windsor Park, where the point earned in the 1-1 draw with Northern Ireland, combined with Denmark's 0-1 defeat in Spain, ensured the Republic went through.

'There was a lot of tension and when Jimmy Quinn scored to put Northern Ireland ahead late on, it looked as though we wouldn't make it until Alan McLoughlin squeezed one in at the near post. We finished before the Denmark match and were watching as they missed a sitter in the last minute which would have knocked us out.'

As a teenager, McGoldrick moved to Kettering and made his Gola League debut at sixteen after playing schoolboy football at Peterborough. He moved to Nuneaton in 1984, where Carr deployed him as a winger, an ironic point in itself as the utility man's conversion to a wing-back and sweeper during 1987-88 ultimately proved the catalyst for his greater advancement in the game. He had to be patient when Hill and Morley made the switch to the full-time ranks in 1985-86 but insisted: 'Graham Carr had always said he would come back for me and that is what happened. The season after he left Nuneaton wasn't a great time but when Telford came in for me, Graham advised me to stay put.'

As in the case of many of his team-mates, Carr's influence on McGoldrick was a profound one, and not just for the fitness schedule, although that remained etched in the mind. McGoldrick was always the star pupil on the long-distance runs at Abington Park, but that didn't exclude him from the odd tongue-lashing. He said: 'Graham would hide behind bushes and creep up from behind. Trevor Morley and Richard Hill would be telling you to slow down and then the gaffer would suddenly appear at your side bawling out: 'Don't slow down and don't listen to them – or you won't be in the team on Saturday.'

McGoldrick vividly recalls a meeting after training one day during 1987-88. He said: 'I was unhappy at not being in the team at the time and I went into the manager's office over the road from the ground. He was sitting with his feet up on the desk, smoking a cigar. I asked him why I wasn't in the team and he told me I wasn't playing well enough and did I want to go on the transfer list? That shocked me and the drive home to Corby that day seemed the longest in my life. The day after that I played in the reserves at Peterborough where I scored a goal and made one. Having won a Division Four championships medal the season before, I thought I had made it, but Graham taught me a valuable lesson and I had a similar experience a few years later at Crystal Palace under Steve Coppell.'

McGoldrick continued: 'Having played in the Conference for five years, I was beginning to wonder whether it would ever happen for me in the league. All that time I was working for a company in Corby called RS Components, packing electrical equipment. When I went to Northampton, Graham Carr was only able to pay me £200 a week. I was on better money during my time at Nuneaton because I also had the day job, but I couldn't afford not take the chance.

Years later McGoldrick and Morley stood on the pitch at Maine Road before fighting out a 1-1 draw late in a season which would see both Crystal Palace and Manchester City earn promotion to Division One. City led Palace in the table by five points at this stage, and were on course for automatic promotion. McGoldrick said: 'We just looked at the magnificent stadium, glanced at one another and laughed. It was a case of remembering where we had been four years earlier playing non-league football and then at the County Ground. Mind you I also remember that Trevor gave me a dead-leg that day.'

It was only after being later converted to a full-back that McGoldrick seized his chance to advance, although the utility tag which he adopted also saw him operate as a sweeper and in the centre of midfield.

Moving to Crystal Palace for £200,000 in January 1989 (his last match for the Cobblers saw him wear the No 5 shirt in a 2-0 win over Bury), he spent four years with the Eagles, making 107 appearances and scoring nine goals. The Selhurst Park deal was sealed ahead of Leicester and David Pleat, after a Sunday dinner spent by the Cobblers player and his wife Margaret with the Coppells. McGoldrick recalled: 'When I joined them in the January we were thirteenth in the table and going nowhere. We went on a run and I think lost only twice in the league up to the end of the season.

Ironically, Morley's late-season goals for Manchester City did enough to haul them over the finishing line, leaving Palace in the play-offs. Morley scored once in a 3-3 draw at home to Bournemouth and again in a 1-1 draw at Bradford City. Despite a 1-0 win over Stoke and a 4-1 romp against Birmingham, Palace ended up with 81 points, a point adrift of City, who only needed a point from their last two games, as they had a superior goal-difference. Palace were denied automatic promotion on the final day when they needed to beat Birmingham 5-0 and hope City slipped up.

The Palace v Birmingham match was a riotous affair with pitch invasions prompted by angry visiting Brummie fans, whose side had been relegated. It caused a delay, although with Palace leading 4-0 inside the first half an hour, their side of the bargain rarely looked in jeopardy.

In the play-offs that followed, McGoldrick played an integral role, after a semi-final 2-1 aggregate win over Swindon. Palace were trailing the first leg of the final 0-3 when McGoldrick firstly pulled one back, before Howard Gayle then missed a penalty for Rovers which would virtually have wrapped it up.

'There were 30,000 people packed into Selhurst Park and, after an Ian Wright opener, the ex-Cobblers winger won a penalty which enabled the Eagles to take it into extra-time. Then came the moment for which McGoldrick is best remembered in Palace folklore, supplying a tight near-post cross from which Wright headed in the winner.

The following Division One season did not turn out to be the dream-ticket McGoldrick had hoped for, as he suffered a torn cartilage in a defeat at Liverpool in the January, ultimately costing him any chance of playing in the FA Cup final that year, a 0-1 replay defeat by Manchester United after the initial showpiece was drawn 3-3. He labelled that as the biggest disappointment of his career.

After spending three years at Arsenal, where he made the most appearances (147) of any of his five league clubs (he also had a spell on loan at Stockport), McGoldrick's switch to Manchester City in 1996 meant following in the footsteps of his old Nuneaton and Cobblers comrade Morley, albeit by a clear seven years.

It had been almost twenty years since a Cobblers player had scored a double on his debut but loan signing Paul McMenemy achieved that three days after the Newcastle defeat on a day when the club created a new club record by netting in 25 consecutive league games, a run going back to the stalemate at Port Vale on the last day of 1985-86.

It proved to be a 'double' day, as the Cobblers scored a first league double of the season with a 5-0 win over Rochdale, managed by Eddie Gray after the sacking of ex-Sunderland Vic Halom. McMenemy's uncle, Lawrie, was manager at Roker Park at the time, although he resigned in the April before the Wearsiders were relegated by the Cobblers' Littlewoods Cup conquerors, Gillingham, in the divisional play-offs.

It was also ironic McMenemy should sign from Upton Park, given he was a temporary replacement for the injured Morley, who would later become a cult hero at West Ham. The double he netted that day emulated Bob Hatton's debut feat for the club against Tranmere in October 1968 but proved to be his only Cobblers goals.

Surprisingly the Cobblers' Rochdale romp was not the best Division Four margin during the afternoon, an accolade which went to Hereford for their 6-0 canter at Burnley, a season's best in the section, matched only by Scunthorpe's 6-0 win over Tranmere the following Saturday.

Before the game, Carr received his second bottle of managerial scotch for being named December's manager of the month, and the season's tempo picked up once more thanks to McMenemy's first-half double, a sixteenth-minute volley and a sweeping 37th-minute strike after Benjamin dummied a McGoldrick cross. Chard, McGoldrick and Hill all added to the tally after half-time, with another Hill effort arguably the pick of the crop, except it was ruled out, with final link man Benjamin in an offside position.

The victory left the Cobblers nineteen points clear at the top of Division Four, and they were now close to their biggest lead of twenty, just seven days away. Behind them, Preston had drawn 1-1 at Swansea when just three matches escaped the weather on 17 January, the Cobblers' scheduled contest at Torquay being one of the casualties. Preston had earned their point with a goal from Nigel Jemson, who scored on his debut at the age of seventeen for the visitors. The Lillywhites then moved into second a week later with a 3-0 win over Lincoln.

If there was ever any doubt the Cobblers' main focus was the league, a second cup exit inside the space of six days confirmed this when the side bowed out of the Freight Rover Trophy on the following Monday evening, with a 2-3 defeat at Fulham.

There was something incongruous about the fact it was the first time the clubs had met since arguably the most important ever contest in Northampton Town's history, the 2-4 home defeat on 23 April 1966 which had all but sealed the side's relegation back to Division Two after one season in the top flight and watched by the biggest ever recorded County Ground gate of 24,523. The return came more than twenty and a half years later in a competition many still labelled 'Mickey Mouse', played out in front of 2,080.

At least the exit door from the competition was nothing if not honourable, as The Cottagers, under the care of Ray Lewington, were a Division Three side. That said, they had been beaten 0-5 at home by Chester two days earlier, a mirror image of the drubbing handed out on the same day by Carr's men to Rochdale.

Gilbert returned after suspension but, on reflection, the highlight of the evening was probably the sight of Carr leaping from the dugout to head a clearance back into play and sending his flat cap flying in the process. The Cobblers side had an unbalanced look and the overall performance didn't match much of what had gone before. Hardly surprising, as you can't deliver five-star performances every time, although the visitors still led entering the final phase.

The evening started badly, at least it did for the Northampton press gang. For one thing, the habitual London traffic meant almost missing the kick-off and to this day, I still count our performance of parking on double-yellow lines outside Hammersmith Police Station and not receiving a ticket as one of the luckiest strokes of my life.

Reed had not enjoyed the happiest Christmas period, having missed five matches over the intensive holiday period through injury, only returning to the line-up at Newcastle. Here, he came in to replace stomach-bug victim McMenemy in attack, partnering Benjamin up front. With Millar again looking vulnerable at left-back against the speed of Gary Barnett, the Cobblers' side overall had an unbalanced look.

Chard cancelled out Kenny Achampong's glorious left-foot drive with a simple headed goal, and Benjamin's diving header after 63 minutes entertained hopes the Cobblers would progress, only for Barnett and John Marshall to strike twice in the final ten minutes.

Changes to the fixture list were becoming commonplace, but at least Cobblers' fans eagerly awaiting the trip to London Road, and the chance to bury the old enemy Peterborough for the third time in a season, only had to make a slight adjustment the following weekend.

The game was initially scheduled for the Sunday, but was brought forward 24 hours to avoid the clash with live television football and the fourth round of the FA Cup. That has always seemed an understandable ploy to me, much more so than the simple line in the 1987-88 *News of the World* Soccer Annual explaining why Montrose were unable to bring forward a New Year's Day kick-off against Airdrie to 2pm. A Montrose official is reputed to have explained: 'There's a sand castle competition at a local hotel and we don't want to clash with such an important fixture.'

The Peterborough match-day programme paid a fitting tribute to the Cobblers' achievements under Carr, quoting memorably: 'Although First Division Newcastle may have inflicted a rare defeat on Northampton when putting them out of the FA Cup last week, back in their own Fourth Division environment it appears an Act of Parliament is necessary to nail the Cobblers.'

Posh manager Noel Cantwell was less gracious about the progress being made 40 miles away. Cantwell's assistant was now Mick Jones, the former Kettering manager who had been in charge at Halifax when the Cobblers' won there 6-3 earlier in the season, but the new London Road management team were unable to stall the Cobblers' juggernaut. While admitting their claim to the top-team title, Cantwell said: 'I don't like their style. They squeeze the game into a 40-yard area by playing the offside trap. Their defence springs out of their half every time their goalkeeper kicks the ball upfield, which I think is boring and unentertaining.'

Fired up by Cantwell's words, the impact on the Cobblers simply fired them up to deliver a third win over the local rivals during the season, albeit by just a 1-0 score-line. Hill (bruised shoulder) and Chard (ricked neck) both shrugged off injuries in their desire to play.

The volume of goalscoring might have been entering a more low-key phase in the season, but the winner on this afternoon was one of outstanding quality and a prime contender for 'goal of the season'. The perpetrator in question was Benjamin, against his old club, and his nineteenth strike of the season was delivered with aplomb in front of Peterborough's best league gate for five years.

The afternoon had entered its 26th minute when Benji received the ball with his back to goal. He turned and nutmegged ex-Cobblers skipper Wakeley Gage in one dazzling move before curling an exquisite left-foot shot in at the far post from a tight angle. It was a stunning replica of his goal against Lincoln, and Benjamin admitted the sweetness was all the greater, coming on the occasion it did.

The rest of the game was less spectacular, played on a bouncing pitch, albeit on a crisp optimistic day. The biggest moment of drama saw Posh physiotherapist Bill Harvey save the life of home full-back Steve Collins who swallowed his tongue after a collision with Gleasure. It provided a scary interlude on an afternoon of sport — at one point the unconscious Collins bit the hand of Harvey, who had once been on the Cobblers' staff, as he performed his act of valour.

In the game, star performances came from Wilcox and Chard in a superbly marshalled defence, but the return journey home allowed the side to reflect on the fact that their lead at the top of the table was now twenty points — at the peak of their powers with the widest margin they would savour during the memorable run.

Two of the division's hot-shots came head to head when the Cobblers drew 1-1 at Tranmere on the following Friday evening, with Ian Muir cancelling out Hill's 51st-minute opener with his twentieth goal of the season. Despite Muir's healthy record though, Rovers were a troubled club, having not won since Boxing Day, and enduring practically the worst home record in the section, while also on the brink of financial collapse. They would part company with manager Worthington in the week that followed, yet their gate of 2,583 was their best of the season.

The Cobblers' goal was a strike which typified their season, a probing ball by Chard producing a flick from the 'masterly' Benjamin, allowing Hill to rifle the ball home. However, it was a more spluttering display, not helped by the fact that Gilbert was sick at half-time, although he soldiered on.

There was no love lost between the Cobblers and Swansea at the time, so it was ironic the 21-match unbeaten league run should come to an end on St Valentine's Day, with the Welsh raiders marching away with a 1-0 victory, earned by a goal two minutes from time by Jason Pascoe.

Records are made to be broken, and this stutter in the season was not only the first home league defeat, it was also the first occasion the Cobblers had failed to score in the league.

The match-day programme for the Swansea game carried a bold rallying 'Now or Never' message about the proposed new stadium from director Barry Stonhill. How ironic this match should be chosen, although in this wonderful season this was a 'one-off' example of the frequently repeated Northampton habit of stumbling on big occasions.

Like Carr, Swansea's manager Terry Yorath had won two gallons of whisky for monthly managerial awards, and like Noel Cantwell, he was no big fan of the Cobblers' style, likening the 'pressing' of the game aspect to American Football, remarking: 'Their main concern is to gain ground. They try to get you to play their way and hit long balls so you fall into the offside trap. However, he did add: 'Northampton are a very good side but never in my wildest dreams did I imagine we would be so many points behind at this stage.'

Swansea scored the only goal when Williams curled over a right-wing cross which Andrew Melville nodded on, allowing Pascoe to head home from a few yards. Both defenders Melville and Terry Phelan went on to greater things during international careers, Melville playing 65 times for Wales and Phelan winning 42 Republic of Ireland caps, while Phelan, Pascoe and Tommy Hutchison all made the PFA's Division Four representative side that season.

Even though the Cobblers were not in a purple patch, it is worth considering Swansea's reaction to this prized scalp on their belt. You might have expected them to march forward valiantly to promotion, yet the opposite proved true. Their remaining seventeen league games brought just three wins, two draws and twelve defeats as they plummeted from third place to twelfth. The Cobblers' form might have dipped, yet they kept plugging on to the winning line.

So Carr's post-match argument still held huge reservoirs of water: 'We've scored 75 league goals this season. What more do you expect?'

CHAPTER SEVEN

Over the Hill and Far Away

Northampton folk are not renowned for their optimism, so the events of 1986-87 were somewhat startling to many residing within the borough. Chairman Derek Banks, being an outsider, did his best to drum up a more visionary approach. After the 2-1 win over Stockport on 21 March, he cracked open a dozen bottles of champagne in the home dressing room, even though technically at this stage, the club hadn't even confirmed promotion.

Banks' reasoning was simple. He was fairly convinced the likes of Swansea and Peterborough, the latter sitting in fourth place at the time, were not going to win the remainder of their games. So, as he was going abroad on business and would miss the next home game, against Orient, when he figured promotion would be won, he didn't want to miss any celebrations. The solution was a simple one. Create your own party! While Banks' reasoning was flawed, it was not fatally so. If his glass remained only half full, that was probably only because he had to drive home to Watford that night.

Contrast this approach to Meccano Stand regular 'Mr Stockport', who was christened by press-box wags at precisely 3.48pm on the day Banks arrived with his Moet & Chandon selection, and when assistant boss Walker was later dumped in the bath fully clothed as high jinks reigned supreme.

It was the last Saturday home game of the season and a stunned air of embarrassment and silence surrounded proceedings as the all-conquering heroes trooped off at half-time in the unfamiliar position of 0-1 down. Wayne Entwhistle was proving a popular chap for the visitors. Not only did he latch onto a Charlie Henry miskick to fire County ahead, he was also presented with a Reed back-pass, only for his shot to be parried by Gleasure. No it wasn't his birthday, he just got lucky on this day.

The players' heads were bent ever so slightly low as they trailed to the relegation candidates. 'Sort them out Carr – bloody rubbish!' came the call from 'Mr Stockport', the heckler who might have resembled one of those ageing gloved puppets, Statler and Waldorf, from the television *Muppet Show*, as he carried out his barracking from the terraces or stand, instead of high up in the theatre box.

That's the trouble with the proletariat – give them something for a while and they then expect a rich harvest as a divine right for almost the next hundred years. Failing that, they start moaning. Ruminating on this philosophy in the bath one night, and with apologies to the great American singer-songwriter Billy Joel, I amended a song version of *Piano Man*:

It's 3 o'clock on a Saturday
    The regular crowd shuffles in
There's an old man sitting next to me
    Waitin' for the match to begin.

He says: 'I know that we're top of the table
    Though I'm not really sure we'll hang on
It might be I'm sad and I should be quite glad
    You'll all regret when I'm gone.'

CHORUS
Bring us a goal, you're the midfield man
    Bring us a goal in spite –
We've been stuck in a right mood of apathy
    But you've got us feelin' alright.

It's a pretty good crowd for a Saturday
    And the manager gives Hill a smile
'Cause he knows that it's him they've been coming to see
    To forget about life for a while.

And the Hotel End sounds like a carnival
    As they sing full of APH Beer
But when Hill hits the bar, they can take it so far
    And troop off to somewhere less dear.

CHORUS (etc, etc)

    For those not familiar with Northampton or the County Ground, which has only hosted county cricket since 1994, APH Beer stands for Abington Park Hotel, a popular hostelry within spitting distance which for many years brewed its own ale, and where a pint or a shed-load of Cobblers could be ordered without in any way decrying the football team.
    As we're dealing with that most frustrating of human traits, namely that of purposefully viewing matters in their dimmest of lights, perhaps it is timely, ironic and somewhat uplifting that the Stockport result was

rescued by two goals from Chard. Five years later he would be asked to run the club's severely weakened playing strength at a time when the words 'financial depression', 'crisis' and 'desperate' were to found in practically every match report. Slaying the dragon against Stockport was probably an easy task by comparison, accomplished by strikes on the hour and again twelve minutes later, the first a direct free-kick and the winner by latching onto a Gilbert cross.

What were we ever worried about? When 'Mr Stockport' returned home to put his feet up and scan the afternoon's football results on that March afternoon he would have realised the Cobblers were in a stronger position than ever, having recovered their half-time deficit while defeats for Preston (0-2 at Cambridge), Peterborough (2-3 at Rochdale) and Swansea (2-3 at Scunthorpe), confirmed Banks' belief that no one behind them would be finishing the season like an express train.

However, the Stockport experience brought another defining afternoon in the history of the Cobblers, for smile as I might at the invasion of unnecessary pessimism, the history books tell us Hill's deal to Watford was all lined up and signed before the following Thursday afternoon's transfer deadline, and Northampton Town's habit of always selling their best players, had closed in on another chapter. Even in such a stand-out campaign, events actually startled few, as the combined rationale of the club's finances and the players' ambition started to tug the best performers away from the mother strings.

Turning the clock back a month, Chard had shone for the Cobblers on a forbidding afternoon in Wolverhampton. It was probably a city best avoided that day, following unrest and clashes in the build-up, and there was sporadic fighting inside the ground involving both sets of fans. Some £1,000 worth of damage was caused at one section of their new multimillion pound stand, which rested uncomfortably in Division Four at the time.

If the locals weren't happy bunnies to begin with, they were incensed after only seven minutes when Chard dispossessed Floyd Streete near halfway, advanced to a position 35 yards out and unleashed the most astonishing blockbuster which screamed into the top corner. It was another outstanding 'goal of the season' candidate from the acting skipper released into midfield thanks to the debut of new Mansfield loan left-back Dave Logan.

For all that, it wasn't a vintage Cobblers performance and Gleasure's heroics in goal protected the advantage three times in the first half when Steve Bull (twice) and Andy Thomson burst clear, breaking the offside line before the veteran Ally Robertson set up Mike Holmes for a second-half equaliser. Carr had still been frustrated in his efforts to sign a new striker, and in many ways lacked quality in depth, causing him to reflect: 'You can't expect the same small squad to go through a 46-match season with a high level of consistency. I am hoping Trevor will be back again soon and that together with a new player we will pick up again.'

Donald or Gilbert was the question which raised its head in the re-arranged match at Torquay on the following Tuesday, when the dilemma of an identity crisis briefly raised its head. True, the pair could both be bracketed as impish midfield players who scored stunning points for consistency at their varying roles, but they offered very different qualities to the cause. Yet it all became a discussion point, albeit a somewhat muted one in the long car journey home, after the 1-0 victory at Plainmoor.

The goalscorer that night was Donald, who had a relatively low profile in a team which had more obvious, rampaging stars in the likes of Hill, Morley, Benjamin and McGoldrick. This was 'Donald the Diligent' who carried out all the donkey work, grafting away in the engine room of the side in a role he neatly summed up years later as 'The Water Carrier', reflecting his task of winning the ball and distributing it to those capable of inflicting most damage to defences. He was always an excellent passer of the ball, and therein lay one of his chief strengths. Donald had few enough opportunities to grab the headlines, and even when he did, the plaudits were almost rudely snatched away from him.

John Robertson was the charismatic radio commentator for Chiltern FM who at the time had Cobblers matches as his seasonal brief. An entertaining broadcaster in his late 50s, with a flair for adding spice and a touch of eccentricity to tales, he offered a certain zany flavour to the press-box. Quick with a quip, I remember him once making a brief study of a match-day programme before announcing in a serious tone: 'I see some Greek is sponsoring the match ball again.' However, all I could find on closer inspection, were the printed words 'anonymous donor'.

At the time, we fondly nicknamed Robertson 'Luke', the reason being quite simple. While his listeners frequently tuned into the Hot FM, the press corps had a tendency to be more world weary and cynical, moderating temperature levels down a notch to simply warm – lukewarm in fact. So Luke it was.

On that particular Tuesday night in Devon, Robertson had shown devotion to duty by catching a train to the English Riviera while I had driven the trusty wagon with an old pal Martin Sargeant for company, taking a well-earned day off from his job with the Northamptonshire constabulary. So rarely did I visit Torquay that it became an essential requisite for us to sample a quintessential English cream tea and scones near the front – except it was February. To this day, I still don't get out very much.

On our arrival at the ground, we were accosted by Robertson, who asked whether we would later give him a lift back, as he was happy to be dropped off at Junction 15, so he could thumb a lift back down the M1 to his home in Dunstable.

This we agreed, and happily settled into our evening routine, Martin and I warmer inside the cramped Plainmoor press-box alongside the Devon hacks, with 'Luke' wrapped up outside, waiting for the action to unfold. We didn't have long for the most significant event of the night, Donald swivelling to fire home the only goal from near the penalty spot after 25 minutes.

The Cobblers held on for a hard-earned victory which stretched their lead at the top to eighteen points and, after gathering post-match quotes from a satisfied Carr, we embarked on the trek home. For me, it meant arrival back at the *Chronicle & Echo* offices at 2am, where I would begin filing my report before the chance to sleep in the following morning. Upper Mounts could be an eerie place in the wee small hours, even while tapping away at the keyboards in the gloom, and on one occasion I distinctly recall almost suffering a heart attack when a fellow employee appeared at my shoulder and asked for an impromptu match report.

Understandably, the conversation home had been stilted during the journey along the M5 and through the Cotswolds, but at one point a half-hearted discussion centred on how a certain individual could pass the evening almost unnoticed, yet grab all the headlines by scoring the winning goal. After a moment a voice from the back seat piped up: 'Just like Dave Gilbert tonight.'

I thought about this one for a moment – sleep deprivation starting to kick in. 'What do you mean, Luke?' I asked after an appropriate pause. 'Surely Warren Donald scored the goal.' The 'safety in numbers' clause kicked in as Martin confirmed my statement.

There followed a short silence before Robertson broke into guffaws of laughter and said: 'That's a funny way to hand in my resignation – I've been giving it out as Dave Gilbert all night!'

Size isn't everything, especially in the case of midfielders in a side intent on hitting its front men early, and anyone casting more than a casual glance at the Cobblers operation during this momentous season must have latched onto that fact in a flash.

With both Gilbert and Donald standing around 5ft 4ins, it was always apparent the pair would be competitive for scraps on the ground, while casting one eye overhead as another cannon ball was launched forward as part of the aerial combat contested up front by attackers Morley and Benjamin.

Perversely, Gilbert wore the No 9 shirt for 142 of his 145 Cobblers league and cup appearances over his three seasons. When you consider the archetypal image of a giant old-fashioned centre-forward in this mould, it perhaps says much about the Cobblers' creation of the unconventional that season.

'I'm obviously not going to win a lot in the air but when it's on the ground . . . ' Gilbert left the sentence unfinished when I interviewed him on the eve of his Cobblers debut at Scunthorpe.

In truth, the secret weapon as far as Gilbert was concerned was using his natural left foot, a quality Carr pounced upon as integral to the success of the side. He explained his strategy by saying: 'When I was at Weymouth I had two natural former left-sided Northampton players in Kevin Dove and Peter Hawkins. Peter played at outside-left before the pair of them went to Bedford and I always had it in my mind about the importance of having those types in the side.'

Gilbert was another classic example of a player grabbing his chance second time around, after being dumped on soccer's scrapheap at nineteen following a disagreement with manager Colin Murphy when Lincoln City just failed to win promotion from Division Three behind Burnley, Carlisle and Fulham in 1981-82.

Gilbert said: 'I was playing in a very good side and when I wasn't playing I was substitute. There were players such as David Felgate in goal, Mick Harford and Trevor Peake. We were only pipped on the final day of the season when we lost to Fulham, who went up instead.' That season, the Cottagers were managed by the former Newcastle and England striker Malcolm Macdonald, although the promotion was overshadowed by the suicide of their defender Dave Clement a few weeks before the end of the campaign.

Gilbert's decision to come to the County Ground wasn't an easy one as he had been top scorer with Boston the previous season with nineteen goals at York Street and added: 'I had a well-paid job so I needed the security of a two-year contract in deciding to come to Northampton. After all, I had four good seasons at Boston.'

The highlight of those was a trip to Wembley for the FA Trophy final in 1985 when Boston were beaten 1-2 by a Wealdstone side who became the first to do the non-league 'double' in that campaign, also successful in the Gola League. His later career was both consistent and inspiring, especially when you bear in mind the early hiccups, for he spent seven years at Grimsby during which time they established themselves as a solid force in the old Division Two, and three years at West Brom after Alan Buckley took him to the Hawthorns.

As we have already pointed out, battling midfield players do not often attract their fair share of headlines, and Warren Ramsay Donald was a case in point. Born and brought up in Hillingdon, his middle name was of Scottish family origin, as his father came from Fife and made no attempt to sound like a British Prime Minister. When he first came to the County Ground on loan from West Ham in March 1985, he shone out like a beacon among a squad of average players during a belated five week flurry which resurrected a little lost faith in the club's fortunes.

The flip-side of the coin for Donald was the fact it meant contemplating severing links with a big London club which had become his home. However, he was becoming desperate for regular first-team football at the age of twenty. He had been on the books at Upton Park from the age of fifteen, having been spotted playing for Hillingdon Sunday League side Mavericks by Hammers scout Charlie Faulkner, who also brought the likes of Alan Devonshire to the club.

Although he only made two substitute appearances for West Ham, both 0-1 home defeats, by Southampton and Everton, he was surrounded by the likes of Devonshire, Trevor Brooking, Paul Goddard, Phil Parkes, Ray Stewart, Alvin Martin and Tony Gayle. 'They were all very good players and I was at the 1980 FA Cup final 1-0 win over Arsenal, which was a great day,' he recalled, adding: 'I also lived in digs with Tony Cottee for four years and the training ground was only ten minutes up the road at Chadwell Heath.'

Donald's penchant for ferocious strikes from long range soon endeared him to the Cobblers' home faithful, bringing as they did goals at home to Stockport and Hartlepool. Perhaps, though, the pinnacle of his range of Exocet-like rockets was the 40-yard stunner he produced at Southend in the 1986 Boxing Day carnival. If ever there was a case of WD40 sparking the battery into life, surely this was it.

Returning to Upton Park after his initial loan period, it did not seem likely Donald would play any significant part under Carr until it dawned on the Cobblers manager those gritty qualities had a place in his side: 'After a few games I realised we could do with a player of his type. Warren used to get through a tremendous amount of work.'

Donald added: 'I could have stayed at West Ham as I was offered a new contract although there was no more money involved, but I was looking to get away and decided to take the gamble.' It helped swing his decision that things were clearly picking up at Northampton under the new regime.'

Donald's initial flurry of goalscoring went into hibernation for a while but when he did hit the target they still tended to be spectacular. His first five Cobblers goals came at home, while the midfielder's next four in 1986-87 all arrived on the road: in the league and cup at Southend, as well as strikes at Halifax and the winner at Torquay.

Later on, his fondest recollections were of a scorching Cobblers volley against a Bolton side including future Hull manager Phil Brown in a 3-0 win in December 1989, when Bobby Barnes hit the other two, and a crisp volley in the twilight of his non-league career at Grantham – ironically enough during a spell at Nuneaton. Donald's love and ability for the game meant he was still turning out at 40 for Raunds Town.

The Donald goal at Torquay left the Devon club just one place off the bottom of the Football League, and indeed, the Gulls would play an intriguing cameo role in this historic season when the bottom club were automatically consigned to what was then the non-league tier, although that is fully detailed later.

Suffice to say that the Cobblers' memories of past re-election campaigns were still rooted deeply in fans' minds. Remember, the club had an unwanted pedigree for seeking re-election or narrowly escaping during the 1970s – it happened twice during the early 1970s and again in 1981-82, when only Scunthorpe and Crewe finished beneath them in Division Four.

Three points from the Torquay match were a more than welcome addition, but from a Cobblers perspective it meant switching attention from 'The Gulls' to 'The Lulls'. Morley's injury was a defining factor, and it would be an understatement to say the season had entered a different phase. A comparison of the next three home games against Halifax, Hartlepool and Scunthorpe, taken alongside the first meetings, fully proved the point.

Those matches inside the space of thirteen days represented the Cobblers 'grind time'. No longer was it possible just to turn up and blast goals past hapless opposition. The new message meant adopting what followers of Bill Shankly and Bob Paisley sides in the 1970s would call the 'Liverpool spirit'. It meant winning 'ugly', winning without playing well, or failing that, scrambling a draw – anything to keep the run going. First time round, the games against Halifax, Hartlepool and Scunthorpe, all away, saw nineteen goals scored at both ends and five points earned. In a whirlwind home spree against the same three, spectators saw only four goals, but a precious seven points were stashed away in the bag.

On 27 February, Halifax were beaten 1-0, but injuries and the odd suspension were making matters tough. Makeshift striker Reed flicked on a

Wilcox free-kick and Benjamin struck at a time it seemed the Cobblers would never score, even though Benjamin had hit a post after only 38 seconds. As the frustration wore on, there were vain cries for handball in the penalty box scattered among goal-line clearances, but it seemed nothing would go in. That was until Benjamin scored. Indeed, the biggest cheer of the whole night had come for the sidelined Morley in the warm-up.

The match programme for Halifax gave ever-optimistic chairman Banks the chance to register his displeasure at the volume of swearing which had manifested itself during the season, notably during an incensed local derby at Peterborough.

Optimistic, because transforming the culture of one small section of football fans is not achieved overnight, simply by the installation of a sign in front of the home 'end'. The 'Gentleman, No Swearing please' board appeared shortly after the London Road visit, and Banks let rip in the Halifax programme, saying: 'The recent match at Peterborough has for me soured a tremendous season. The bunch of cretins who caused trouble before, during and after the match have spoiled the good reputation we have created over the last two years and brought shame on the club's name, its staff and supporters. I hope their families are proud of them, because nobody else is.'

Morley was still not ready for the Wednesday night match against Hartlepool for which Chard, who had hobbled off against Halifax on crutches after getting a kick on the knee, then began a two-match ban. Donald missed the next pair of games against Scunthorpe and Cambridge due to suspension, the result of totted-up bookings.

The only obvious similarity with the 3-3 November draw by the North Sea was the presence of Roy Hogan once again appearing on the scoresheet. He struck for the visitors after beating the offside trap in the third minute, only for Benjamin to equalise before half-time. For once, all the domination was counting for nothing, a fact reflected in a combined corner-count of 31-6 over two home matches, but nothing to show for those flag-kicks at the sharp end. The fact that Preston ended Exeter's unbeaten home record 2-1 at St James Park on the same evening meant the lead at the top was reduced to fifteen points.

The following Saturday brought an unexpected break. I remember the travelling press corps reaching a pub on the outskirts of Worcester before a phone call revealed what the snow had threatened after a pitch inspection at Edgar Street. Carr's men would not be facing Hereford that afternoon. Call it suspicious if you like, but the Bulls had lost their previous six games, and danger-man Stewart Phillips would have been suspended for this one.

It was a pattern which was starting to emerge, and when the Aldershot visit was called off at the end of the month, the Cobblers had seen no fewer than nine matches called off during the season, including the four cancellations of the Newcastle Cup-tie. From the original fixture list back in the summer, another three weekend matches shifted by 24 hours, while the Scunthorpe home game had initially been scheduled on FA Cup third round day.

The Cobblers' resources were still stretched, and Carr's efforts to sign a loan midfielder were thwarted before the visit of Scunthorpe on the following Wednesday, the negative impact of which was trampled underfoot by the return of Morley.

The humorous streak which ran through the Carr family meant you never quite knew when certain individuals were being serious – was the real reason for the absence of new blood really the fact a rival manager had taken his team camping and had remained stubbornly out of reach in the days before mobile phones?

Basically, it didn't matter. The night was one of those rare occasions when someone up on high had read the script. Sixty-six minutes had elapsed of a panic-riddled affair against Scunthorpe when Morley latched onto a loose ball in the box and nodded a winner. The Hotel End went wild, well fairly pleased anyway.

Far more upbeat was the local derby tussle with Cambridge three days later, which brought a no-nonsense 3-0 win at the expense of a side who arrived at the County Ground with four wins and five straight clean sheets. Six would have made a club record for the U's, yet it proved mission impossible for the visitors.

Finally heartened by the arrival of fresh legs – Charlie Henry making his debut on loan from Swindon – the Cobblers were fired up on a glorious spring day and were ahead by the eighteenth minute, Gilbert despatching one of a brace of afternoon penalties, the first awarded after a handball from Alan Kimble.

Hill's strike eleven minutes before the break settled the issue, sent clear from halfway by a combination of Chard and Morley to beat Keith Branagan. It was his first goal in seven games and his 50th for the club.

Elsewhere in the section, the strain was starting to show on Swansea, whose manager Yorath made a brief playing comeback at the age of 37 as his side conceded three goals in the final thirteen minutes at Wolves in a 0-4 loss. At a national level, most attention was hooked on the four FA Cup quarter-finals, where history was made with each of the away sides coming out on top for the first time in the competition's history, namely: Watford, Coventry, Leeds and Spurs.

Henry scored his only goal in a Cobblers shirt on the following Tuesday evening, but it proved a below-par effort, the side slipping to a 1-2 defeat at Turf Moor against a Burnley team which would endure their fair share of anguish over the final six weeks of the season. It was Budget Day, and an occasion for cuts everywhere. While Chancellor Nigel Lawson took a snip at income tax, Preston made minor inroads into the lead, cutting it back to seventeen points with two games in hand, thanks to a 3-0 win over Stockport, Gary Swann opening things up after just fourteen seconds.

For Henry at least, the penalty-box strike recalled fonder goalscoring moments, although Cobblers fans preferred not to think about his winner at the County Ground in 1985-86 when he ended up as the Robins' leading marksman.

While the Cobblers were rectifying the slight blip at home to Stockport four days later, midfielder Mann was making his Torquay debut on loan in a 4-2 win at Halifax, in which Paul Dobson went haywire with all the Gulls' goals, in his side's first away win of the season. Mann went on to make six starts at Plainmoor, as well as a couple of substitute appearances.

The stage was set for breaking news, with transfer deadline day confirming that hotshot Hill would be moving to pastures fresh, but not until the end of the season. Hill had missed the Stockport match, the only occasion he would fail to start a Cobblers game all season, but conspiracy theorists were silenced by the fact that the midfield man was serving a one-match suspension. Yet movements were definitely afoot, Carr had been trying to bring Corby-born striker Dave Longhurst back to his home county from Halifax all season. Although it would have offset any immediate loss of Hill, the Cobblers boss would have to be patient a while longer.

Hill recalled his day his destiny and a future career with Watford and Oxford. He said: 'I was still in bed when Graham Carr rang me around 7am. He told me to put my suit on and get to the County Ground as we were going out for the day.'

Even this simple instruction could have been a problem, especially in the early days, as he explained: 'I don't know what it was about Northampton and the County Ground but I should think for the first two or three weeks I came training there after signing from Nuneaton I never went the same route twice. I remember once winding a window down by the Cock Hotel junction in Kingsthorpe and asking a postman for directions and even he didn't know. I thought "what sort of a town is this, if no one knows where the football club is"?'

Hill and Carr's initial appointment was with John Hollins at Chelsea, who were to finish in the bottom half of Division One that season. However, negotiations did not go as smoothly as either party might have wished, although the Northampton player denied any greed on his behalf, citing the massive north-south divide in the property market as his sticking point.

While at Stamford Bridge, Carr took a call from the Northampton offices and once outside told Hill: 'We are calling in at Watford on the way home.'

The transformation at Vicarage Road was immense, Hill claiming: 'From the moment I walked in I felt at home. It was if the girls on the reception desk had been told I was the new signing but, as I found out, that's how they were anyway. Graham Taylor was eloquent and honest, and both he and Eddie Plumley, the chief executive, were a different class. They were preparing for an FA Cup semi-final with Tottenham at the time but they made me feel very at home.'

The transfer saga did not completely end there, for after returning home and popping the champagne corks with his wife Elaine and parents Keith and Dorothy, Hill had an even earlier phone call the following morning. Taking up the tale, he said: 'It was around 6.30am and I thought the voice sounded familiar.' The caller turned out to be none other than Spurs boss David Pleat, with Hill recalling: 'He asked me why I had just signed for Chelsea which was what had been in the morning papers. I told him I had actually signed for Watford.'

The irony of the situation, as it transpired, was that although the Hornets deal was struck to most people's satisfaction, a club-record transfer fee of £258,500 being agreed, with Hill allowed to finish the season at Northampton, Graham Taylor moved to relegated Aston Villa in the June and was replaced by Dave Bassett.

Despite a 'do you still want him?' telephone call from Carr being answered in the affirmative, Hill's Watford career did not pan out smoothly. He quickly moved on, in company with David Bardsley, to Oxford, managed by Maurice Evans, with Glyn Hodges going in the opposite direction. Hill's curious claim to fame in 1987-88, and not one he tries to sweep under the carpet, is that he played for two relegated clubs in one season, as Watford and Oxford finished at the bottom of the pile.

Horse racing had long been one of Hill's other sporting passions, so perhaps there was irony attached to the fact that his first match after the Watford deal had been dusted was the Friday night top of the table shindig in Lancashire at Preston, nine miles from Aintree, which would play witness to a success for 28-1 winner Maori Venture in the Grand National on the following day.

Certainly the Preston programme notes took up the theme. The Lilywhites were unbeaten at home since 4 November, so it was appropriate that an excerpt read: 'Tomorrow is the Aintree horse racing spectacular and tonight is the football equivalent – the clash of two thoroughbreds in the peak of condition.'

Hill and the Cobblers drew a blank, going down to a tenth-minute strike by Gary Brazil, although Wilcox had what looked a perfectly legitimate headed goal from a Gilbert corner ruled out, while Benjamin's crisp 75th-minute volley was tipped onto the bar by Alan Kelly.

No matter, the Cobblers had still proven their pedigree, on this their baptism on a plastic pitch. Club photographer Norton stopped over in Lancashire, and the next day spent five hours waiting by Becher's Brook for Lean Ar Aghaidh to lead the field round on the first circuit.

While the likes of Carr, Donald and Hill were among the principle Cobblers of the time who loved having a bet, perhaps it would have been too much to expect three points at Preston and backing the Grand National winner to boot.

Besides, the Cobblers' red-letter day with the horses had come almost eighteen months earlier after the morning 2-0 kick-off win at Colchester. To Hill, it proved the players were living some sort of 'golden dream', a period which you experience only once in your life.

Hill recalled: 'That day at Colchester I think we were in the bar by 1pm and left Layer Road at about 4.30pm. The director Don Hammond used to put bets on with a bookmaker in Hinckley and that day he had four horses which we all backed, and which all came in. We didn't know the results until they came over on the radio when we were on the way home. The first one won and then the second and the whole business on the coach started to get more out of hand. By the time the fourth one was given out the coach was rocking all over the place and I'm surprised we stayed on the road. We won a good deal of money – I'm not sure how much but I remember once going round Don's house with £1,000 so it can't have been trivial.'

Hill's lesson for life is to make hay during the magical times. He added: 'I don't think I've had four winners in a Lucky 15 bet since.'

CHAPTER EIGHT

Swings and Roundabouts

In the summer of 1987 the golfer Nick Faldo showed extraordinary calm and resilience during the final round of the British Open Championship played at Muirfield in East Lothian to come of age in a 'major' tour event and win by one shot from Paul Azinger.

Comparisons between golf and Division Four title-winning outfits are perhaps not that common. Certainly, it wasn't a huge preoccupation or diversion in the County Ground dressing room that year. 'We didn't really have any big golfers but Chard was probably the best,' one of the players told me.

Yet the Cobblers could be likened to the triumphant Faldo in the sense they were in the act of 'breaking through' a barrier to success as unlikely, untouted heroes, even though they led most of the way and ultimately went on to win by a healthy points margin.

In both instances it was a case of holding nerve entering a critical final phase. Maintaining a mental strength, as well as possessing a physical one. Talk to your average club golfer who has just re-entered the club house after experiencing a tough and testing back nine holes in the face of a howling gale, and you might begin to understand the finale of the Cobblers' 1986-87 campaign. On the third day Faldo's Open was played in conditions so wet and windy that four holes were shortened in distance so players could reach the fairways from the tees.

On the final round he became a 'par machine' to break Azinger's heart. In the Cobblers' case, the finishing line and the Division Four Championship was in sight, yet none of the large field of opposition was making it easy for them. Their own run-in proved that with the odd stumble and lapse into the rough and the gorse bushes, but like Faldo, they kept grinding away, especially at home.

Super fitness, a near perfect balance to the side, coupled with individuals who possessed both flair and battling win qualities in equal measures had always looked like ensuring the ends would justify the means. Yet to a degree, the efforts and energies had taken their toll.

Morley's return during the second week of March meant it wasn't just the clocks going forward once more. Yet the odd below-par performance had crept into the Cobblers' make-up. When the back nine arrived it was no longer a case of staring an eagle pointedly in the eye and taking a pop at the odd albatross. Still, it made an historical change from having such a massive bird draped around your shoulders, dragging you certainly to your doom. A birdie was a joy, while walking off the 18th with a par, would do 'just nicely thank you'.

To their credit, the last nine matches brought four wins, two draws and three defeats to ensure the job was done in a respectable manner. Seventeen goals scored, but sixteen conceded. Importantly, performances at home stood up to all the battering. Bouncy Northampton pitches in March and April had frequently proved the club's undoing in the past, tempered by liberal buckets of sand. Sometimes taking a corner by the Spion Kop could be like chipping out of a bunker, although nothing could have been more traumatic than the time Gilbert stepped back to address a corner-kick at Bolton's Burnden Park ground a few years later and disappeared down into the moat surrounding the pitch. Thankfully, most of the hard work had already been done.

The rearranged trip to Hereford on 8 April was not an occasion to waste many paragraphs when revelling in the club's weightier achievement, but it did indicate levels of rising pressures and temperatures in the boiler room. This manifested itself in a *Chronicle & Echo* headline the next day which read 'What a Load of Rubbish'. Somehow you wondered whether 'Mr Stockport' had changed vocation and begun a series of clandestine shifts working on the sub-editor's desk at Upper Mounts.

With hindsight, it seems an incredibly damming piece of journalism to inflict on a team which had achieved what the Cobblers had done over the previous 37 league matches. There is small doubt it was their worst performance of the season, with the only miracle they were not beaten more severely than the 2-3 margin, and the previous month had proved it was not a 'one-off' on their travels. Even so, they didn't deserve that. High expectation levels, perhaps coupled with a perverse sense of wit, were perhaps to blame.

The Cobblers were lucky not to be trailing before the Bulls took the lead in the 25th minute, Stewart Phillips spurning two great chances after Gleasure made an excellent flying one-handed save from the striker's header. Instantly after falling behind to Phillips, Chard levelled things with a cool finish (perhaps applied with a putter-like precision) tucked inside a post after Benjamin had held the ball up. Offside appeals were then in vain as Steve Spooner made it 1-2 before the break. Even that could have read worse as Phillips rattled a post but the contest was apparently wrapped up when Ollie Kearns struck in the second half.

Hereford proceeded to squander yet more chances before Morley netted a goal of high quality in injury-time, volleying into the top corner, yet was too embarrassed to celebrate after the dirge preceding it. Ironically, at the death, a couple of mini-breaks for the Cobblers could even have rescued a point on a nadir night.

It was never going to be a great occasion for quotes from the manager and immediate post-match analysis, and the same could be said of the following contest four days later when the Cobblers restored the equilibrium and defeated Leyton Orient 2-0 on a Sunday afternoon at the County Ground. The win was achieved with Gilbert's first outfield goal of the season, struck by his unfavoured right foot, and a McPherson header from a Donald cross.

The relationship between a reporter on an evening newspaper and his club manager can be a fraught one at the best of times. On the one hand, 'the boss' has to win all the psychological games with his players and perform a delicate juggling act to help guarantee performances on the field. Meanwhile the hack needs to constantly deliver a crop of worthwhile stories and an honest assessment of what is going on.

I take plenty of satisfaction from the fact that 25 years after these events, I can say I have happily communicated with Graham Carr on a fairly regular basis, all the more rewarding when you consider the wider path he has trodden. We have sat together in cars before funerals in reflective mood as well as sharing jokes in hospitality boxes at the races, also laughing hysterically together at examples of the family's noted wit.

Mind you, he doesn't ask my opinion on player-strengths too often and I would be stretching truth to an impossible extent to say it was always sweetness and light during my four years on the road with the Cobblers under Carr. However, we both worked at it, which I believe is the test of any relationship.

I once remember driving home from a defeat at Blackpool thinking it was an incredibly long way to go to be given a two-worded quote that couldn't possibly be reproduced in a family newspaper, but these experiences were exceptions rather than rule and now pass as 'water under the bridge'. On the other hand, even watching awful games, while part and parcel of the job, can have their moments. I remember the ultimate abysmal goalless draw at Wigan in September 1989, Carr's last season at the Northampton helm. It was a 'defend and be damned' afternoon. Twenty minutes after the final whistle the press-gang came face to face with Messrs Carr and Walker on a sunny afternoon outside Springfield Park. We all stared at one another for a few seconds and then everyone burst into spontaneous laughter. It had all been so forgettable, there was simply nothing you could say.

Certainly I didn't know everything, nor in many ways would I have wanted to. Yet I was dealing with people's livelihoods and many of my sometimes 'off the cuff' comments would have been picked up and taken as 'gospel' by avid readers and those close to the running of the club.

Managers and teams come under all sorts of pressure, while many a reporter's task and life has been made a misery not by the words he has written, but the screaming headline sitting uncomfortably at the top of the page and never to be erased, at least in that edition.

Looking back on all this, let's just say it is not surprising that the Orient report contained only a quote from visiting manager Frank Clark. After the Hereford headline, regardless of whether I had written it, this was a cool week in the Beesley-Carr relationship. Meanwhile Clark conceded the Cobblers were worthy winners while lamenting the fact his side overdid the football approach. 'I thought we were trying to walk it in during the first half. Too many of my players were crowded out in the second half and if you can't stand up to that, you get found out by teams like Northampton. They are a credit to the division and they have earned promotion and the title. I hope they get it.'

Defender Dave Logan had been signed by Carr in February at a time when he had been pursuing a striker as cover for the injured Morley. He is not to be confused with the American Footballer for the Cleveland Browns, although there is little doubt the Carr network could comfortably have stretched across the North Atlantic had it so wished.

The timing of such a move would have been typical of the manager's 'throw them off the scent' policy, except for the fact he had been bugged all season by the fact he was missing a natural left-sided full-back. In fact it was coincidence it should happen now. Chard and loan signing Gernon had more than manfully filled in, but it was a case of opportunity knocks when the chance came up to acquire Logan for £20,000 from Mansfield. While the move was not a wholesale disaster, and the Middlesbrough-born player made 41 appearances before switching to Halifax the next season, it soon became apparent Logan arrived with 'baggage' which manifested itself in a *Chron* headline 'Why I sent Logan home'. It's safe to say the new arrival did not adhere to all the rules set by the club.

Still, his presence left Chard free to further explore his 'versatile' tag, wearing the numbers: 10, 4, 11, 3 briefly again, and 9 shirts before the end of the season, so Logan's presence had benefits, although goalscoring had been in nobody's mind until the trip to Colchester on 17 April.

Although the match brought one of only two Cobblers' defeats all season by more than one goal, the performance was more in keeping with their league standing. Logan's sweet early strike from a Gilbert free-kick had apparently set them up, after the left-back had been brought down on the edge of the box, dragged himself to his feet and executed his own form of retribution. It made him the fifteenth player to hit the target with everyone bar goalkeeper Gleasure having now scored. Yet Richard Wilkins equalised for the U's before half-time. Nicky Chatterton's penalty after Wilcox felled Tony Adcock from behind then made it 2-1, and Rudi Hedman tapped home for 3-1 when Adcock's header was touched onto the bar by Gleasure.

Southend faced Carr's men for the fourth occasion this season on the following bank holiday Monday evening, and again the Cobblers held the whip hand, executing a 2-1 win to leave them within three points of mathematically clinching the title. The Cobblers had not lost to Southend in seven meetings under Carr, and the night also established a seasonal club record of nineteen home league wins.

Hill's first goal in over a month and a McPherson header put the Cobblers twelve points ahead of Preston with five matches remaining, third-placed Shrimpers now a further eight points behind, one ahead of Wolves, whose late run was still in full momentum. Both goals arrived from set-pieces, Hill stabbing home after his initial header from a Gilbert corner had deflected back to him via Chard's boot, while McPherson headed in a Gilbert free-kick three minutes after the break. Southend's late consolation came from Richard Cadette. It was his penultimate goal of a season in which he hit the target 31 times, 24 of them in the league, five of them against the Cobblers.

McPherson's two goals in three games were a bonus at a stage of the season when the side were beginning to show the odd crack. Yet it was typical that among the Cobblers' three representatives in the PFA Division Four side that season he should stand up and be counted, as he had done all season alongside Russell Wilcox in the heart of the defence.

The PFA representative side, which also included Hill and Morley, was this: Stannard (Southend), Parris (Peterborough), Phelan (Swansea), McPherson (Northampton), Allardyce (Preston), Hill (Northampton), Harvey (Hereford), Hutchison (Swansea), Cadette (Southend), Morley (Northampton), Pascoe (Swansea).

Of McPherson's nine Cobblers' goals in five years, only that from Gilbert's cross at Crewe in November 1986 was achieved with a boot, which in a succinct way summed up the former West Ham defender's abilities in the air, where he was awesome, and on the deck, where he was not. Never the best passer of the ball, his aerial domination was immense and once Wilcox came into the side after missing the first nine league games through injury, they forged a great partnership in the centre.

McPherson's career highlight was playing for Reading in the epic Division One 1995 play-off final against Bolton, his only appearance at

Wembley. Reading had won English football's third tier a season earlier, and then finished runners-up to Bryan Robson's Middlesbrough. They were forced down the play-off road due to the streamlining of the Premier League, which meant only two promotion places. Reading had defeated Tranmere in the semi-finals, with Bolton accounting for Wolves. While the Royals had Shaka Hislop in goal, Bolton's substitute goalkeeper was Peter Shilton! McPherson was playing with a broken foot and his side were 2-0 up at half-time, but Reading also missed a penalty which proved to be a turning point. They were dragged into extra-time, where they trailed 2-4 before pulling back a late consolation to lose 3-4.

McPherson had been a member of West Ham's FA Youth Cup winning side of 1981, his only senior Hammers appearance bringing the curtain down on the 1984-85 season with a 0-3 defeat by Liverpool at Upton Park. It wasn't quite a case of: 'Well if I'm expected to mark Ian Rush every week that's it, I'm off to Northampton!' but it might have been. Besides, he managed to fit in a loan spell at Cambridge first.

McPherson's post-Northampton career meant nine years at Reading under Ian Porterfield, Mark McGhee, Jimmy Quinn and Mick Gooding, and Tommy Burns, before finishing at Brighton between 1999-2000, when Micky Adams and Alan Cork held the managerial reins. The Reading period brought several reunions with Wilcox, the occasion being Division One contests against Hull, as Wilcox was a player at Boothferry Park for three years, then moving on to Doncaster, Preston and Scunthorpe where he ultimately switched into management.

Wilcox said: 'Macca was great in the air and I like to think my strength was in my reading of the game. The other thing about Keith was that he knew his weaknesses which some players quite often don't, so he wouldn't try things he couldn't achieve.'

McPherson said: 'When I signed for Northampton, Graham stressed the importance of staying locally, so although I still lived in London I would be here for a couple of nights before a match. I was caught out on the odd occasion when I stayed over in London on a Friday night. I remember once driving up in hurricane conditions on a Saturday which made me late and knowing Graham would realise what I had done.'

In fact, McPherson's Northampton 'digs' were with a lady in Stanhope Road, Anne White, whose son John was a keen Cobblers fan. The close contact remained when the defender became godfather to his son, Ben.

Both Wilcox and McPherson had lengthy Cobblers stints, making over 150 (Wilcox) and 200 (McPherson) appearances. Yet in something of a hare and tortoise cameo, a glance at the final league playing records of the 1986-87 season make fascinating reading. Wilcox was the last

Cobblers player to play in the league, being substituted for Scunthorpe in a basement match at Southend on 23 March 2002, a match the Shrimpers won 2-0. That showing meant his appearance tally ticked over to 501, one ahead of McPherson who made his final outing, number 500 for Brighton on 29 April 2000, when he came on as a substitute in a 2-1 win at Shrewsbury.

Both Wilcox and McPherson provide examples of players who blossomed at the County Ground before moving on to distinguished careers elsewhere, although while the former switched into a coaching and management capacity after hanging up his boots, principally as an assistant boss to Brian Laws with Scunthorpe (where he finished his playing career), Sheffield Wednesday and Burnley, McPherson retrained at college in IT and quickly moved into employment in that capacity at an independent school in Reigate.

Ironically, when Carr brought Wilcox to the County Ground in 1986 the player turned down the chance to go to Wednesday, a decision he admitted flabbergasted some of his best mates at the time. Mind you, as he had already been turned away as a young pro by Doncaster and Cambridge, the reasoning was sound. 'I took the broader view and thought I might get lost at a big club like Wednesday.' And, of course, Carr sold the Cobblers to him, strongly emphasising the need to be local to the club where you were playing.

Wilcox recalled: 'When he signed me, I remember Graham driving me around some of the better areas of Northampton and telling me to buy a property. He said: "You need to be doing something now." The point was, prices were going up £1,000 a month at the boom time.' A slight hesitation by the player only brought the same response from Carr: 'Now!'

Carr knew Wilcox well enough from the non-league circuit but watched him play in two non-league internationals with Northern Ireland at Nuneaton and Kidderminster. Both brought 2-1 wins for the England side and Wilcox scored in the Manor Park match. At this time, Wilcox's old Frickley team-mate Reed used to forewarn him when Carr would be watching, so he could make sure he wasn't sporting the ear-ring the scout in the stand disapproved of.

The terror of Monday mornings spent running round parks and rugby pitches still flickers in their minds, but both emphasised the role played by coach Walker, who was both a sergeant major when the square-bashing took place, but a mental shrink later in the dressing room. 'He was the one to pick you up and have a laugh,' said Wilcox. 'As someone who later spent plenty of time as a number two, I think I now appreciate Clive's role much more. Graham would suddenly pop up behind players without you realising he was there. Someone might start moaning about the training and the next thing you knew the gaffer would be bawling in your ears, something like: "You'll be thanking me when you get your win bonuses on Saturday"!'

Wilcox and McPherson were both in the Cobblers side on 26 April when it was all expected to be done and dusted at Lincoln. Six straight Sunday wins: against Torquay, Peterborough in league and cup, Lincoln, Cardiff over Christmas, and Leyton Orient, had been interlaced at regular intervals through the season, so the prospect of travelling to Sincil Bank for the return with the Imps appeared friendly enough, with the prospect of clinching the Division Four title the carrot at the end of the stick. Set against that was the fact that the Cobblers had now lost their previous four on the road: at Burnley, Preston, Hereford and Colchester. Something had to give, and sadly, from a Cobblers' perspective, it was the Sunday best sequence.

It was a sunny, blue-sky day, and the press-box uniquely situated behind the goal gave splendid views of the city's cathedral, set on top of the hill. According to at least one historical point of reference, it is the most outstanding piece of architecture in the British Isles.

For some reason I can't put my finger on, the other point of interest was the fact that the local Lincoln City reporter was named Julie, a quite unusual phenomenon in those days. Perhaps Julian or Julius popped up on the Division Four circuit, but certainly no Julies.

As it turned out, I would probably have been better served by delving into the Lincoln Tourist Guide and noting interesting facts such as: 'reputedly the tallest building in the world between 1300 and 1549' (which is just about the time the half-time whistle blows if you have a football fan with a 24-hour clock). No doubt some 2,000 travelling Cobblers fans wished they had entertained similar notions. On that day, thank goodness for the blue sky, sunshine and the sight of Julie and Lincoln cathedral. Anything but the football!

The script was going haywire after only eight minutes when Jimmy Gilligan, father of future Cobblers player Ryan, scored his only goal in a Lincoln shirt, chesting down a cross in a suspiciously offside position before winning the leap for the ball with Gleasure, the ball rolling apologetically into the net.

Carr spent several moments that day with his head buried in his hands, Ally MacLeod style, and Lincoln secured only their second win in fourteen starts, and their final victory before briefly dropping out of the League, helped by a Willie Gamble strike and a freak Chard own-goal. Turning to hook a mighty back-pass from just inside his own half, Chard watched dismayed as his massive swing saw the ball sail over Gleasure and into the net. He later recalled: 'I used to tell Gleasure that was the only time he came off his line all season!' A consolation strike from McGoldrick merely reversed the score at the County Ground.

The Cobblers' final home game, against Crewe, came on the Wednesday evening. This was 24 hours after Preston had beaten Tranmere 2-0 at Deepdale to move to 85 points and reduce the lead at the top to six with three games remaining.

The Lincoln defeat meant the tension was heightened for the visit of Dario Gradi's Railwaymen, who, as has already been mentioned, included future England stars Platt and Thomas in their ranks.

I should point out at this juncture that any accurate references gleaned from my report of the 2-1 win in the following evening's *Chronicle & Echo* should be treated with some scepticism. The reason for this is straightforward as, unbeknown to me, part of the planned celebration was dumping the local football reporter fully clothed in the team bath.

In fact, two of my stand-out County Ground memories surround the phrase 'Team Bath'. In December 1992, during a 3-0 FA Cup second round replay with Bath City, I proudly donned my boots at half-time and scored all three of my penalties for a media team in front of the Hotel End against then youth-team stopper Delroy Preddie. I puffed my chest out with pride and the night became a 'dining out' conversation piece for some time to come.

However, my first Bath night and the absence of a change of clothing meant a decidedly soggy note-book went back to Upper Mounts that night to file copy. This is why I am known as 'The Memory Man', a facet I appear to have acquired from my grandfather, Bill Beesley, who I barely knew before he died in 1965. He used to write a column recalling great Cobblers matches stretching back to the 1920s in the *Chronicle & Echo*.

The class of 1986-87 knew or cared nothing about this, and why should they? When recalling the soaking in a phone conversation with Hill years later, he pointed out I clearly didn't have a change of clothes (how many season-ticket holders arrive with a three-piece suit on the off-chance the roof might spring a leak?). I complained: 'I could have died of pneumonia!' to which he replied: 'Not a chance – 1986-87 was our golden age and nothing ever went wrong.' That was a comfort then!

Luckily, the most salient facts of the night were easy to commit to memory and the report began: 'Champagne cascaded on to wildly ecstatic Cobblers' fans as Graham Carr's crowned heroes took a rapturous bow and toasted a deserved championship success in high style at the County Ground last night. Players lined the back of the stand and revelled in a carnival atmosphere, free of the nervy fetters which had cast a mood of pessimism over the final weeks.' Don't think I missed anything there.

However, the important points are that skipper Morley's habit of taking the odd theatrical stumble in the box had not deserted him, crashing under a challenge from John Pemberton. This allowed Gilbert to stroke home a 24th-minute penalty, low inside Brian Parkin's left-hand post.

There was also an entirely fitting farewell home strike by Hill nine minutes after the restart, which meant that a late consolation by former Coventry and Manchester City midfielder Peter Bodak was simply that, causing me to reflect why I had forgotten to bring my bottle of Vosene as I took the plunge.

Hill's typically precocious strike led to a race back to halfway where he was greeted with a bear-hug from boss Carr, as I reported that night – 'the man who has made it all possible'.

Three matches remained, and with promotion and the title clinched, two targets remained to cap a phenomenal season. In both cases it was a matter of reaching the magical 100. Six points and four goals became the twin ambitions, all within the space of six days and all away from home.

The mission began at Cardiff's Ninian Park on a bank holiday Monday. Early progress was made, Benjamin netting after receiving a Chard cross and turning sweetly to fire in, although this was not to be the finest hour of home goalkeeper Mel Rees who was possibly unsighted.

However, after former Leeds and Swansea striker Alan Curtis equalised, both Rees and Gleasure performed heroics in the closing stages to keep the score at 1-1, Gleasure's point-blank stop from Paul Wimbleton after 85 minutes a contender for save of the season. How he stopped it was anyone's guess, that he actually clung onto the ball was nothing short of a minor miracle. The draw ended a run of four straight away defeats.

Two days later the venue was Aldershot's Recreation Ground, where a change of goalscoring luck was required after just two goals in ten visits, the winless streak stretching back to the early 1970s. Of course, the class of 1986-87 didn't know any of this, or if they did they couldn't care less. How else do you explain a 3-3 draw? Three times the Cobblers pulled themselves back from a deficit in the rescheduled clash, Gilbert, Morley and Benjamin doing the trick on the night Paul Bunce made his debut as a substitute, having arrived from Leicester as squad cover.

However, the fact the Cobblers had drawn successive matches meant the 100-point target was now out of their reach in advance of the final match, at Wrexham, where the match programme respectfully listed the Northampton team underneath the word 'Champions' on the back page.

8. SWINGS AND ROUNDABOUTS

More significant issues were being settled elsewhere, but the Cobblers ended their most memorable season for 21 years (the never to be forgotten Division One campaign) on a high note with a 3-1 win. The home angle on the day was that Newport were relegated from Division Three, which meant that, for the first time, all four Welsh league clubs – Wrexham, Swansea, Cardiff and Newport – would be playing in the bottom section next season. Southend won 2-0 at Stockport, earning them promotion with the Cobblers and Preston, consigning Wolves, Aldershot and Colchester to the play-offs, alongside Bolton, who occupied 21st position in Division Three.

However, the real drama of the day was at the other end of the table and the desperate scramble to avoid becoming the first club to drop out of the league automatically and be demoted to the Conference. At the sharp end was a Cobblers loan-out player, as Aidy Mann played a key part in Torquay's dramatic injury-time survival special at Plainmoor which resulted in Lincoln being ousted from the Football League.

Mann made six loan appearances at Torquay in March and early April as Carr sought to help his old mate, Gulls manager Stuart Morgan. Mann briefly returned to the County Ground but came off the bench to play in each of Torquay's last two matches, a 2-3 defeat at Orient and the 2-2 draw with a Crewe team once again involving Platt and Thomas.

The circumstances surrounding Torquay's survival is a classic mixture of the unpredictable and bizarre. Prior to the final weekend, Burnley propped up the Football League, with Torquay one place above them. Lincoln, who headed to Swansea to wrap up their season, needed the fates to conspire against them, with Tranmere also placed between them and the trap-door. However, a late Friday night winner for Rovers at home to Exeter made it a three-way fight going into the Saturday.

While the Cobblers were easing down the gas at Wrexham, Burnley leapt from the foot of the table with a 2-1 win over Orient, while Lincoln were beaten 0-2 at Swansea.

Matters looked bleak for Torquay, especially as they trailed 0-2 at home to Crewe at half-time, with both goals scored by Bodak. Right-back Jim McNichol pulled a goal back in the 48th minute, just as Burnley were grabbing a second against Orient, which would ultimately secure their safety, but McNichol was then involved in a bizarre drama which ultimately secured the Gulls' league lifeline.

After clearing the ball up the touchline, sliding into advertising boards in the process, McNichol was bitten on the thigh by a German shepherd police dog named Bryn. Bryn presumably thought the Scot was about to attack his handler, posted close at hand to react to any pitch invasion on the final whistle, a not unlikely scenario given the Gulls' desperate plight. During the four minutes injury-time created by McNichol's ordeal, it became apparent that Lincoln had fallen 0-2 behind (after 80 minutes) and Torquay could survive by earning a draw, which they duly did with a goal by Paul Dobson in the third minute of stoppage time.

Local lad Mann had entered the fray at half-time and his memory of events is still clear: 'Jim McNichol came off the pitch after he was bitten by the police dog and was heavily strapped up before coming back. Yet there was a lot of blood and it reminded me of Terry Butcher's headband against Sweden in 1989. It wouldn't have been allowed nowadays.'

Mann added: 'I remember hitting the crossbar in injury-time and Paul Dobson scoring. It was like pandemonium on the pitch and Stuart Morgan spoke to the crowd on a microphone. If I remember rightly Jim McNichol was on BBC television on *Wogan* on the Monday night, where he met Bryn the police dog and stroked him!'

The irony for Mann was that after leaving Northampton for Newport, he was out on loan at Wycombe at the end of the following season when Lincoln clinched their immediate return to the Football League. Just as twelve months earlier, when the Imps hit bottom spot for the first time on the final day, they went on to clinch the 1987-88 Conference title by reaching the summit for the first and only time at the death following a 2-0 victory over a Wanderers side including Mann, in front of a record crowd of 9,432.

If ever clubs needed a lesson on not resting on their laurels, Lincoln's example was surely it, though Northampton's own murky past teaches us this is not always taken on board. The Imps experience of 2010-11 proved yet again history repeats itself – even 24 years down the line.

So, a remarkable chapter of events. On New Year's Day 1987, ten days after being defeated 1-3 at the County Ground, the Imps stood seventh in Division Four. On 26 April they would beat the Cobblers 3-1 at Sincil Bank; their last win before a brief sojourn in the Conference.

The following season when the Cobblers' failed to make the Division Three play-offs, the Imps won the Conference. Kettering, then managed by Alan Buckley, were five points behind in third. That Kettering side included three players – Paul Curtis, Russell Lewis and Mark Schiavi – who had been released by Carr at Northampton. They looked like lifting the title when beating Lincoln 2-0 with three matches left. However, they then lost a fifteen-match unbeaten run at Runcorn and failed to secure another point. The next time Kettering came so close to gaining league status was under Carr, with Northampton a whisker away from heading in the opposite direction.

CHAPTER NINE

The Watford Connection (II)

There are occasions in life when the radar to which we all adhere seems ever so slightly faulty. Just the merest adjustment appears necessary, the odd tweaking of the dial. The evening of 25 June 2011 was a classic case in point in Northampton, with a prominent clue in the number 25.

As the 25th anniversary of the Division Four championship season loomed large, a somewhat rare and major reunion had been planned for many of its principle participants, but not at the County Ground, the most logical stage, if harking back to the heyday of 1986-87. Even so, the Watford Connection was on everybody's lips there on the same night, as the Cobblers' old home buzzed and rocked to the sound of one old football club chairman, in the form of Sir Elton John.

'Saturday Night's Alright For Fighting?' Certainly not at the Tollemache Arms at Harrington, where Graham Reed's 50th birthday celebrations were in full swing a day after his landmark date. A marquee was erected in the pub garden with a hog roast for those feeling a little peckish. Glorious views over a green county, the best of Northamptonshire. So, unless the odd skittle went astray in the games room (and let's face it 'Rambo' Reed's aggression these days is focused on hurling down cheeses for his local pub team), a civilised night was in store.

Had you taken that fifteen-mile drive north from the County Ground to Harrington that evening you would have discovered a man who once had Northampton, Watford and football engrained in his heart. Derek Banks, whose cash investment ignited the 1986-87 charge, returned to the county. An occasion almost as rare, if less feted than that of the musical knight of the realm where 15,000 assembled. Here surely though, was Northampton Town's version of *Rocket Man*.

It was possible to split the night down the middle and combine two parties, with Chard, for one, achieving that feat. Still, what else would you expect from the utility man of the side? In his typically down to earth manner, Reed had laid foundations stones. 'I've invited them all and now it's up to all of them what they do with it,' he told me a week beforehand. Of course, not everybody turned up. It just doesn't happen. Richard Hill had the best excuse as far as I could gather. A few days earlier he had set off again chasing soccer's pot of gold at the end of the rainbow once more, teaming up again with his old mate and fellow ex-Cobblers' legend John Gregory, to coach FC Kairat in Kazakhstan for a year.

Perhaps not a *Yellow Brick Road* in the case of a player whose 33 goals almost overhauled the record of 39 amassed for Northampton by Cliff Holton in league and cup in 1961-62, but a Red Route in any case, which meant no stopping or pausing for breath. Curiously, Holton's place of birth is given as Oxford, where Hill went on to play after Watford, while the one-time Arsenal legend had two spells with Watford, the club for which he left Northampton in December 1962. It is also worth noting Richard and Elaine Hill named one of their sons Daniel (the other is Gary) though I suspect there was no thought of Elton John song titles in the process.

The attendance sheet still read: Carr, Walker, Casey, Reed, Morley, McPherson, Donald, Chard, Schiavi, Gernon, Benjamin and Chard, as well as my old photographic side-kick Norton, who inevitably enjoyed a typical 'busman's holiday'. Many is the time he has been offered a free pork roll and crackling on production of his camera, in return for a willingness to carry on snapping.

Midway during the evening, almost with a beat of drums, there was a turn of heads in the car-park to a figure who brought instant recognition. The inevitable onset of middle-aged spread maybe, but still the perfect English gentleman. Derek Banks was soon at home, whisky clutched safely in one hand, as though he had never been away. It was all slightly surreal. Banks had been desperate to make the gig, despite a function in Reading that afternoon, which meant a chauffeur on overtime. This at least meant he was able to enjoy hospitality to the full before 'crashing' at nearby Great Cransley.

'It was a brilliant evening. The memories I had just flooded back instantly,' he said. 'Everybody had fond recollections of that time and it seemed like I had never been away. It is one of those events I will never forget – up there with winning the league. The guys have turned out brilliant and they looked splendid with their wives – a real tight and happy bunch and I shall tell you this. If I ever did venture anything again in any shape or form, I would be down there and involve the lot of them! I was so proud of them and what they have become. As I write this I am sitting in Hong Kong looking over the bay and wondering the same thing. Instead of hanging around there for a couple of days and accepting the various invitations I had to leave and get a flight to China – too much rushing around and for what?'

Banks was always a generous man, with his family-based financing of the club in 1985 setting the ball rolling. Benjamin recalled: 'My wife Annabelle and I were married in the summer of 1986 and we were practically broke at the time. I spoke to the chairman and he told me to come down and see him in Watford. He met me at the station and we went for a ride in a taxi. He gave me £800 in an envelope there and then. I have never forgotten that, although Derek did initially when I reminded him. It slowly came back as we talked.'

Other players recall the eel-skin wallets Banks personally gifted to each member of the first team, which stood the test of time. Having heard this tale from several mouths, I secretly wished they had been crocodile. It would have been appropriate. *Crocodile Rock* was the first single I ever bought, in 1972, and while I would like to have heard Sir Elton John banging it out at the County Ground, I know I was in the right place that evening. On reflection, eel-skin wallets make sense. They remind me of pre-match saunters along Southend promenade with jellied eels on sale at the stalls. Back in those days, we always had Southend in our pockets.

Again befitting the man, Morley proved a star turn, flying from Norway to attend, although he also owned a property in Loughton which admittedly helped. I had long wanted to ask him about his sending-off in a televised match between Manchester City and Aston Villa on 22 October 22, 1989. Also given his marching orders at the same time was Villa's Stuart Gray, a future Northampton manager. This is what football historians like to call 'ironic' (albeit with historical hindsight).

Morley happily related the incident, while admitting it was not one of his prouder moments. His mum Jill had asked him to be on his best behaviour for the cameras. It seems he elbowed Gray in the face but was not slow in hitting the deck himself when the Villa skipper made a subtle response.

Villa boss Graham Taylor took Morley to task, although Morley recalled: 'I think Ron Atkinson was the TV pundit and portrayed me as the innocent victim.' Morley so nearly had a Watford connection himself. He was all set to follow the same initial path as Hill in January 1988 when Dave Bassett was sacked at Vicarage Road and the deal was called off. Morley moved to Manchester City a fortnight later.

Of course, the players all eventually moved on. While sad, it is all the more vital we cling to memories. Players must seize the moment. In the final throes of research, I witnessed Frankie Belfon, the hero of a famous 1982 FA Cup victory, outside his house preparing for the next day's refuse collection. 'Just think', I reflected, 'that great night putting out Gillingham and now, all these years on, putting out the wheelie-bin.'

Years later the whole championship business almost seemed a dream, but better that than the scenario portrayed by comedian Stan Boardman when the staff enjoyed a night at the Derngate Theatre in Northampton in 1985, a few years after its opening. 'I hear the Cobblers' vice-chairman

Stuart Wilson passed out the other day while shopping in the town centre,' began Boardman. 'When Stuart came round after a few minutes he found himself being attended in a building society.' 'Where am I?' asked a clearly shaky Wilson. 'Don't worry – you're in the Alliance,' a helpful member of staff told him. Visibly disturbed, Wilson responded after a few seconds: 'Whatever happened to the Fourth Division?'

I don't expect that sketch will ever find its way onto Alan Carr's script, and it is stretching a point to accept he unearthed any material during those half-term holidays in 1986 reading *Peril At End House* by Agatha Christie at the County Ground (for this was indeed the fiction under his scrutiny and fittingly something we reveal in the final chapter.).

Still, as the Cobblers leapt from the dead in the mid-1980s under Carr senior, it is appropriate that a character in that Christie tome is Jim Lazarus, who marries Freddie Rice, an odd name for a heroine. Alan's father has never shown the same penchant for Christie novels but if he ever gets bored on a scouting flight to Europe, I recommend 'Passenger To (Eintracht) Frankfurt'.

In the weeks that followed the final league match at Wrexham, the Cobblers' championship triumph was set off by celebrations in the town, although at that time no one was splashing cash too wildly. This was proven when the final whistle went at The Racecourse, causing a euphoric Hill to remove his shirt and throw it among the band of followers, presenting a problem. 'We stopped up there for a friendly at Bangor the next day so we had to get it back again,' recalled Carr.

On Monday, 19 May an open-topped double-decker bus cruised from the County Ground and along the town's Wellingborough Road to the Guildhall, players waving to all and sundry along a ten-minute journey for a civic reception. Euphoric scenes at journey-end were remarkable for those who imagined the good folk of Northampton simply didn't care or know a good team when they saw one.

At the height of the revelry, club secretary Dr John Evans said: 'Not even the great Brazilians of the 1970s have given me as much pleasure as this side.' At that moment, chairman Banks, in a random act of generosity, handed over the Today Trophy to the town's Mayor, Cllr Cyril Benton. Taken aback, he described a marvellous gesture and said: 'I see football like a lift, constantly going up and down. All we have to do now is disconnect the down button.'

That's easier said than done, Mr Mayor. For as we all know in Northampton, after a season in the sun comes a decade in the shade.

GUIDE TO SEASONAL SUMMARIES

Col 1: Match number (for league fixtures); Round (for cup-ties).
e.g. 4R means 'Fourth round replay.'

Col 2: Date of the fixture and whether Home (H), Away (A), or Neutral (N).

Col 3: Opposition.

Col 4: Attendances. Home gates appear in roman; Away gates in *italics*.
Figures in **bold** indicate the largest and smallest gates, at home and away.
Average home and away attendances appear after the final league match.

Col 5: Respective league positions of Cobblers and opponents after the game.
Cobblers' position appears on the top line in roman.
Their opponents' position appears on the second line in *italics*.
For cup-ties, the division and position of opponents is provided.
e.g. 2:12 means the opposition are twelfth in Division 2.

Col 6: The top line shows the result: W(in), D(raw), or L(ose).
The second line shows Cobblers' cumulative points total.

Col 7: The match score, Cobblers' given first.
Scores in **bold** show Cobblers' biggest league win and heaviest defeat.

Col 8: The half-time score, Cobblers' given first.

Col 9: The top line shows Cobblers' scorers and times of goals in roman.
The second line shows opponents' scorers and times of goals in *italics*.
A 'p' after the time of a goal denotes a penalty; 'og' an own-goal.
The third line gives the name of the match referee.

Team line-ups: Cobblers' line-ups appear on top line, irrespective of whether they are home or away. Opposition teams are on the second line in *italics*.
Players of either side who are sent off are marked !
Cobblers' players making their league debuts are displayed in **bold**.

Substitutes: Names of substitutes appear only if they actually took the field.
A player substituted is marked *

N.B. For clarity, all information appearing in *italics* relates to opposing teams.

LEAGUE DIVISION 4   Manager: Graham Carr   SEASON 1986-87

No	Date		Att	Pos	Pt	F-A	H-T	Scorers, Times, and Referees	1	2	3	4	5	6	7	8	9	10	11	12 sub used
1	23/8	A SCUNTHORPE	2,302	7	1	2-2	2-0	Hill 5, Reed 10 Cammack 60, Hunter 62 Ref: P Harrison	Gleasure Green	Reed Russell	Chard Longden	Donald Money	Coy Lister	McPherson Hunter	McGoldrick Birch	Gilbert Cammack	Benjamin Johnson	Morley McLean	Hill* Stevenson	Schiavi
2	31/8	H TORQUAY	3,558	4 20	W 4	1-0	1-0	Benjamin 44 Ref: R Wiseman	Gleasure Smeulders	Reed McNichol	Chard King	Donald Cann	Coy Compton	McPherson Richards	McGoldrick Musker	Benjamin Crowe	Gilbert Walsh	Morley Nardiello	Hill Dobson*	Pyle
3	6/9	A ROCHDALE	1,556	4 19	W 7	2-1	1-1	Benjamin 23, Chard 67 Taylor 32 Ref: P L Wright	Gleasure Redfern	Reed Johnson	Chard Grant	Donald Smart	Coy Bramhall	McPherson Gibson	McGoldrick McHale	Benjamin Taylor	Gilbert Shearer	Morley Mills	Hill Conway	
4	14/9	H PETERBROUGH	5,517	1 16	W 10	2-1	2-0	Morley 4, Chard 41p Gregory 76 Ref: I.Hemley	Gleasure Beasley	Reed Paris	Chard Collins	Donald Gunn	Coy Price	McPherson Gage	McGoldrick Christie	Benjamin Fuccillo	Gilbert Lawrence	Morley Gallagher	Hill Luke*	Gregory
5	17/9	H TRANMERE	3,857	1 9	W 13	2-0	1-0	McGoldrick 9, Hill 80 Ref: D Phillips	Gleasure O'Rourke	Reed Mungall	Chard Hughes	Donald Thorpe	Coy Moore	McPherson Vickers	McGoldrick Morrissey	Benjamin Bell	Gilbert Muir	Morley Bullock	Hill Anderson	
6	20/9	A SWANSEA	6,902	2 1	L 13	1-2	1-1	Chard 45 McCarthy 39, Love 52 Ref: R Hamer	Gleasure Hughes	Reed Harrison	Chard Melville	Donald Lewis	Coy Phelan	McPherson Emmanuel	Hill Hough	Gilbert Hutchison	Gilbert McCarthy	Morley Love	McGoldrick* Pascoe	Mann
7	27/9	H WOLVES	5,731	1 18	W 16	2-1	2-0	Morley 16, Hill 29 Match 57 Ref: M James	Gleasure Nixon	Reed Oldroyd*	Chard Barnes	Donald* Street	Coy Zelem	McPherson Robertson	McGoldrick Lockhart	Benjamin Stoutt	Gilbert Match	Morley Handysides	Hill Edwards	Holmes
8	30/9	A HALIFAX	1,034	1 24	W 19	6-3	3-1	Don'd 5, Ben' 20, Hill 43, 47, 87p, Ch'd 75 Brown 8, Holden 53, Longhurst 53 Ref: K Lupton	Gleasure Gregory	Reed Brown	Chard Thornber	Donald Martin*	Coy Knill	McPherson Galloway	McGoldrick Saunderson	Benjamin Nicholson	Gilbert Black	Morley Longhurst	Hill Holden	Matthews
9	4/10	H ALDERSHOT	4,303	1 19	W 22	4-2	1-2	Hill 7, 76, Morley 61, Chard 72 Langley 12, Ring 14 Ref: K Morton	Gleasure Lange	Reed Blankley	Chard Mazzon	Donald Wignall	Coy Anderson	McPherson Shrubb	McGoldrick Ring	Benjamin Burvill	Gilbert Foyle	Morley McDonald	Hill Langley	
10	17/10	A CAMBRIDGE	6,285	1 8	W 25	3-2	1-2	McPherson 40, Chard 57p, Morley 70 Cooper 33, Crown 42 Ref: A Ward	Gleasure Branagan	Reed Measham	Chard Dowman	Donald Beattie	Wilcox Smith	McPherson Beck	McGoldrick Flannagan*	Benjamin Spriggs	Gilbert Cooper	Morley Crown	Hill Schiavi	Littlejohns
11	22/10	H BURNLEY	5,718	1 12	W 28	4-2	3-0	Morley 26, 37, Benjamin 43, Hill 66 James 64, Hoskin 85 Ref: T Holbrook	Gleasure Neenan	Reed Rodaway	Chard Hampton	Donald Kennedy	Wilcox Gallagher	McPherson Deakin	McGoldrick Grewcock	Benjamin Britton	Gilbert Parker	Morley James	Hill Hoskin	

1 Reed scores on the opening day for the second season running, but this time playing as a full-back. The last time a Cobblers' full-back scored on the opening day it was Barry Tucker's deflected 45-yarder in the first minute at Huddersfield in 1975-76, and promotion was the end result.

2 Gulls' goalkeeper John Smeulders provides some Sunday eccentrics, including a late flare-up with Gilbert when he attempts to strangle the Cobblers' midfielder. Smeulders is at fault for Benjamin's goal, supplied by a McGoldrick pass as both he and Gilbert make home debuts.

3 The Cobblers had won only one of their previous nine visits to Spotland (losing six) so this victory was a welcome indication of the barometer swing. After Bramhall hit a post and Shearer missed a sitter inside eight minutes for the hosts, it was relatively plain sailing for Carr's men.

4 The Cobblers went top of a division for the first time in ten years with this Sunday win over the derby rivals, with Benjamin and Chard meeting their old club. Posh had ex-Cobblers Wakeley Gage and Derrick Christie who arrived at London Road after spells with Cambridge and Cardiff.

5 Rovers player-boss Frank Worthington named himself on the bench but only got as far as removing his tracksuit bottoms. Rovers had pulled back a 2-0 lead in the closing stages ten months earlier to draw, but there was to be no repeat as Carr's men edged two points clear of Preston.

6 The Cobblers' unbeaten league run of seven matches comes to an end ... but the reaction would prove immense. Swans' boss Terry Yorath is proving an instant success by taking his side top of Division Four after moving from his role as assistant manager at Bradford City in July.

7 The attendance to see fallen giants Wolves is the biggest since 6,464 rattled through the turnstiles for the visit of Peterborough in December 1983. It is the best attendance in Division Three and Four, also higher than four in Division Two – Grimsby, Oldham, Millwall, Shrewsbury.

8 This was the first time the Cobblers had scored six goals away in a league match since the 6-2 win at Walsall, in February 1931. The Shaymen ended with the joint worst defensive record in the division (with Burnley) and they also went down 3-5 at Rochdale in their penultimate match.

9 An eventful afternoon for Chard who misses the chance to make it 2-2 with a first-half penalty and is knocked out cold in the second, but still recovers to take his goal tally to five from full-back. Cobblers recover to celebrate boss Carr's Manager Of The Month award for September.

10 Benjamin makes his 100th league appearance but it is McPherson, against his old club, who keeps the side in the hunt before Chard and Morley send the Cobblers five points clear. It is Cambridge's biggest crowd since Kevin Keegan's visit with Newcastle United in his farewell year.

11 Nineteen goals in five games, but attack-happy Cobblers waste at least as many chances again in a frenzied assault. Benjamin stars despite his having recent x-rays for a back injury, responding to speculation over an approach for Chester's Ian Richardson which threatens his place.

154

12 H HEREFORD 25/10 — 5,336 — W 3-2 — 18 31
Gleasure, Reed, Chard, Donald, Wilcox, McPherson, Benjamin, Gilbert, Morley, Hill
Rose, Rodgerson, Dalziel, Halliday, Cegielski, Delve, Harvey, Phillips, Kearns, Butler
Morley 6, Benjamin 8, Hill 21
Phillips 67, Devine 82
Ref: D Elleray
On this day, Jim Melrose scores the season's fastest goal (nine seconds before Charlton at West Ham) and the Cobblers strike early before easing their grip in the second half. Stewart Phillips' late 'equaliser' is ruled out for offside. Swansea are in second place after the 5-3 win at Torquay.

13 A STOCKPORT 27/10 — 1,729 — W 3-0 — 24 34
Gleasure, Reed, Chard, Donald, Wilcox, McPherson, Benjamin, Gilbert, Morley, Hill
Farnworth, Evans, Mackenzie, Lester, Matthewson, Wilkes, Entwhistle, Allatt, Bailey*, Mossman, Mitchell
Hill 35, 48, Morley 89
Ref: J Watson
Jimmy Melia's men are in an appalling run of form (no victories between 19 September and 22 November) and in this month also lose 0-10 on aggregate to Sheffield Wednesday in the Littlewoods Cup. The Cobblers go ten points clear, although Donald's booking will mean a ban.

14 A HARTLEPOOL 1/11 — 1,626 — D 3-3 — 23 35
Gleasure, Reed, Chard, Donald, Wilcox, McPherson, Benjamin, Gilbert, Morley, Hill
Blackburn, Nobbs, McKinnon, Hogan, Smith, Honour, Lowe, Turner, Walker, Dixon
Chard 20p, Hill 22, 85
Hogan 9p, Dixon 24, Wilcox 66 (og)
Ref: L Dilkes
Chard becomes the second Cobblers' player on the tot-up booking system, meaning he will miss the Peterborough FA Cup-tie. Hogan is a hero turned villain, turned hero again, as he converted a spot-kick, then handled for Chard's equaliser, only to deliver a free-kick for Dixon's goal.

15 A LEYTON ORIENT 4/11 — 3,496 — W 1-0 — 13 38
Gleasure, Reed, Chard, Donald, Wilcox*, McPherson, Benjamin, Gilbert, Morley, Hill
Wells, Sitton, Mountford, Foster, Harvey, Cornwell, Castle, Brooks, Jones, Fishenden, Comfort*, Sussex
Benjamin 13
Ref: J Martin
It is a momentous few days for football, as later in the week Manchester United will appoint Alex Ferguson to replace Ron Atkinson. The Cobblers are still eight points clear at the top as Swansea beat Cambridge 2-0, but 13 points ahead of Colchester in fourth spot.

16 H PRESTON 8/11 — 6,537 — W 3-1 — 6 41
Gleasure, Reed, Chard, Donald, Wilcox*, McPherson, Benjamin, Gilbert, Morley, Hill, McGoldrick
Brown, McNeil, Bennett, Atkins, Jones, Allardyce, Williams!, Thomas, Taylor, McAteer, Hildersley
Benjamin 33, McPherson 65, Hill 87
Taylor 45
Ref: K Cooper
Steve Taylor scored against the Cobblers for Rochdale earlier in the season, but his equaliser is a mere irritation as the County Ground crowd hits another new high spot, and Hill's late goal is a vintage effort. Wilcox goes off with double vision and Germon switches roles on his debut.

17 A CREWE 28/11 — 2,331 — W 5-0 — 15 44
Gleasure, Reed, Chard, Mann, Wilcox, McPherson, Benjamin, Gilbert, Morley, Hill, McGoldrick
Parkin, Pemberton, Macowat, Wright, Davis, Goodison*, Platt, Puller, Cutler, Milligan, Jarvis, Chapman
Benjamin 12, McPherson 16, [Hill 29, 73, 86] McGoldrick 35, Hill 38, 72
Ref: T Simpson
Crewe's Tuesday match at Preston had been cancelled due to flu and illness, and they were left looking even sicker as a 500-strong Cobblers following relished this Friday night cracker. Hill's tally of 18 goals is the highest in the country and the lead at the top is ten points once more.

18 H EXETER 2/12 — 6,639 — W 4-0 — 6 47
Gleasure, Reed, Chard, Mann, Wilcox, McPherson, Benjamin, Gilbert, Morley, Hill
Shaw, Batty, Viney, Marker, Priddle, Watson, Harrower, Joyce*, Roberts, Keogh, Biggins, Kellow
Morley 17, McGoldrick 35, Hill 38, 72
Ref: N Butler
The Grecians failed to win away from home all season but this romp was impressive, given the fact Exeter had conceded just 11 goals prior to the fixture. Counter-acting the offside trap, Exeter ensured they were caught as far forward as possible, buying them time and space to defend.

19 H WREXHAM 13/12 — 6,070 — D 2-2 — 4 48
Gleasure, Reed, Chard, Donald, Wilcox, McPherson, Benjamin, Gilbert, Morley, Hill
Pearce, Salathiel, Cunnington, Williams, Cooke, Comstive, Massey, Horne, Steel, Charles, Conroy
Wilcox 54, Benjamin 84
Steel 33, 65
Ref: J Brady
The headlines after this rare slip were more about interest shown by Liverpool in goal-ace Hill, although he failed to add to his tally of 22. The Robins' Steve Charles marked Hill, having performed a similar job on a Spanish international in their recent European tie with Real Zaragoza.

20 H LINCOLN 21/12 — 7,463 — W 3-1 — 7 51
Gleasure, Reed, Chard, Donald, Wilcox, McPherson, Benjamin, Gilbert, Morley, Hill
Swinburne, Hodson, Buckley, Daniel, West, Strodder, Cooper, Simmons, Lund, Mitchell, McInnes
Gilbert 41p, McGoldr'k 54 Benjamin 75
Lund 24
Ref: J Barratt
Highest league gate watch The Imps' early impetus, inspired by left-winger Ian McInnes, wear off. Gilbert keeps his 100 per cent penalty record, against his old club, while Lincoln boss George Kerr says: 'I think Northampton are promoted, and two sent off it was more a Boxing Day skirmish. Four trips to Roots Hall in little more than a year had seen the Cobblers score a stunning total of 15 goals.

21 A SOUTHEND 26/12 — 8,387 — W 4-0 — 2 54
Gleasure, Chard, O'Shea, Johnson, Martin, Roberts, Hall, Clark, Pennyfather, Cadette, McDonough!, Maddix
Hill 38, 70, Benjamin 44, Donald 83
Ref: A Buksh
Southend won 2-1 at Wolves six days earlier, so this 11.30am clash was billed as a Christmas cracker but with eight booked and two sent off it was more a Boxing Day skirmish. Four trips to Roots Hall in little more than a year had seen the Cobblers score a stunning total of 15 goals.

22 H CARDIFF 28/12 — 11,138 — W 4-1 — 10 57
Gleasure, Chard, Ford, Wimbleton*, Brignull, McPherson, Boyle, Platnauer, Bartlett, Pike, Vaughan, Marustik, Curtis
Benj'n 4, Gilbert 38p, Morley 74, Hill 76
Pike 33
Ref: M Cotton
Goalkeeper Graham Moseley, who had been in goal for Brighton in the 1983 FA Cup final against Manchester United, was sent off early on for hauling down Hill outside the box, and although Michael Ford was not disgraced as a deputy, there was only one winner from that point on.

23 H COLCHESTER 1/1 — 8,215 — W 3-2 — 8 60
Gleasure, Reed, Chard, Gernon, Phillips, Hinshelwood, Wilcox, Day, Donald, Baker, McGoldrick, Benjamin, Lowe, Farrell, McPherson, Adcock, Pike, Morley, Wilkins*, Hill, English T, Norman
Benjamin 49, Morley 57, Gilbert 85p
Adcock 52, 61
Ref: D Vickers
Stubborn resistance is overcome as the Cobblers triumph after twice being pegged back. Alec Chamberlain, who later moved to live in Northampton, got both hands to Gilbert's sixth penalty of the season, but couldn't stop the ball bouncing up and into the net for the winner.

LEAGUE DIVISION 4 — Manager: Graham Carr — SEASON 1986-87

No	Date		Att	Pos	Pt	F-A	H-T	Scorers, Times, and Referees	1	2	3	4	5	6	7	8	9	10	11	12 sub used
24	3/1	A EXETER	4,331	1 8	D 61	1-1	0-1	Hill 59 Biggins 38 Ref: A Seville	Gleasure Shaw	Chard Harrower	Gernon Viney	Donald Marker	Wilcox McCaffrey	McPherson Taylor	McGoldrick Batty	Benjamin Robson*	Gilbert Biggins	Morley Keogh	Hill O'Connell	Kellow
								The Grecians demonstrate exactly how they manage to draw exactly half their league games, equalling a record of 23 set by Norwich in the 1978-79 season, although the Canaries only played 42 matches in Division One. It has since been matched by both Hartlepool and Cardiff.												
25	24/1	H ROCHDALE	5,484	1 23	W 64	5-0	2-0	McMenemy 16, 37, Chard 52, [McGoldrick 55, Hill 65] Hill Ref: J Lovatt	Gleasure	Reed Redfern	Millar Johnson	Donald Grant	Wilcox Bramhall	McPherson Smart	McGoldrick Reid	Benjamin Conning	Chard Stanton	McMenemy Woods	Hill Parlane	
								The Cobblers equal a club record by scoring in 25 consecutive league games — a 0-0 draw at Port Vale on the last day of 1985-86 was their last blank. Hereford's 6-0 win at Burnley is the biggest win of the season in this division, matched a week later by Scunthorpe against Tranmere.												
26	31/1	A PETERBOROUGH	7,911	1 13	W 67	1-0	1-0	Benjamin 26 Ref: G Napthine	Gleasure Shoemake	Reed Paris	Chard Collins*	Donald Nightingale	Wilcox Price	McPherson Gage	McGoldrick Luke	Benjamin Fuccillo	Gilbert Gallagher	McMenemy Phillips	Hill Kelly	Gregory
								The Cobblers have the 'Indian sign' over the old enemy. Noel Cantwell is critical of the Cobblers' style, saying: "Since I came back, I have noticed a difference in the way the game is played. There are more offsides, everything is so much tighter and quicker. There is no room."												
27	6/2	A TRANMERE	2,538	1 18	D 68	1-1	0-0	Hill 51 Muir 75 Ref: G Ashby	Gleasure Farnworth	Reed Thorpe	Chard Hay	Donald Williams	Wilcox Mungall	McPherson Vickers	McGoldrick Morrissey	Benjamin Bell	Gilbert Muir*	McMenemy Hughes*	Hill Anderson	Worthington
								Rovers hadn't won since a Boxing Day success at Rochdale and included loan goalkeeper Simon Farnworth, beaten by the Cobblers three times at Stockport in October. While Hill hit his 30th goal of the season, it was Muir's 22nd. The Cobblers' top scorer also hit the woodwork.												
28	14/2	H SWANSEA	8,288	1 3	L 68	0-1	0-0	Pascoe 88 Ref: K Walmsley	Gleasure Hughes	Reed Harrison	Chard Phelan	Donald Hough	Wilcox Emmanuel	McPherson Melville	McGoldrick McCarthy	Benjamin Lovell*	Gilbert Williams	McMenemy Pascoe	Hill Hutchison	Andrews
								Well it had to happen at some time … the unbeaten and consecutive scoring sequences comes to an end, with the lead cut to 17 points. Carr's men even collected their first bookings since Boxing Day, Chard and Benjamin earning cautions. This is hardly a cause for mass panic though.												
29	21/2	A WOLVES	9,991	1 8	D 69	1-1	0-1	Chard 7 Holmes 59 Ref: K Cooper	Gleasure Kendall	Reed Stoutt	Logan Barnes	Donald Thompson	Wilcox Clarke	McPherson Robertson	Mann* Purdie	Benjamin Streete	Gilbert Bull	Chard Match	Hill Holmes	McGoldrick
								The goals have dried up and Carr is seeking a replacement striker, with the injured Morley badly missed. No surprises that the Cobblers' strike is an absolute screaming 25-yarder from Chard, which flies into the top corner. Wolves' star is in the ascendancy, just one loss in five games.												
30	24/2	A TORQUAY	1,780	1 23	W 72	1-0	1-0	Donald 25 Ref: K Cooper	Gleasure Allen	Reed Richards	Logan Kelly	Donald Dawkins	Wilcox Cole	McPherson McNichol	Mann Gardner	Benjamin Henry	Gilbert Walsh	Chard Nardiello*	Hill Holloway	Coy Muster
								An excellent three points in the context of the season. The Gulls might have diced with disaster until the final seconds of 1986-87, but they only lost seven of 23 at home and this came at a time when the Cobblers' engine was misfiring. Ian Holloway starred on the wing for Torquay.												
31	27/2	H HALIFAX	6,351	1 15	W 75	1-0	0-0	Benjamin 83 Ref: D Reeves	Gleasure Whitehead	Reed Brown	Logan Fleming	Donald Matthews	Wilcox Sword	McPherson Galloway	McGoldrick Farnaby*	Benjamin Martin	Gilbert Black	Chard* Diamond	Hill Nicholson	Coy Barr
								The first Friday night home game since March 1981 when the Cobblers drew 3-3 with Scunthorpe, thanks to a Peter Denyer hat-trick. Coy's substitute appearance is a first since the Gillingham Freight Rover Trophy tie. Preston are 18 points behind, but do have two games in hand.												
32	4/3	H HARTLEPOOL	5,470	1 20	D 76	1-1	1-1	Benjamin 36 Hogan 3 Ref: I Hemley	Gleasure Blackburn	Reed Barrett	Logan Nobbs	Donald Hogan*	Wilcox Smith	McPherson Stockle	McGoldrick Toman	Benjamin Borthwick	Gilbert Dixon	Reed Walker	Hill McKinnon	Shoulder
								Preston's 2-2 draw at Wolves on Saturday had cut the deficit to 17 points but two more were eroded as John McGrath's sided ended Exeter's unbeaten home record on this night, winning 2-1 at St James Park. Thirty-one corners earned in two home games, but none produced a goal.												
33	11/3	H SCUNTHORPE	5,352	1 15	W 79	1-0	0-0	Morley 66 Ref: D Hutchinson	Gleasure Green	Reed Russell	Logan Longden	Mann Harle	Wilcox Hunter	McPherson Smith	McGoldrick Birch	Benjamin Money	Gilbert Johnson	Morley Flounders	Hill Lister	
								The cream of the north London management school, unbeaten in six, yet were swept away by an upbeat display which was reminiscent of early season. 'Baden Powell' stand – so called because it is always full of scouts. The Iron had lost five of their previous six matches and it was modest fare.												
34	14/3	H CAMBRIDGE	6,201	1 9	W 82	3-0	2-0	Gilbert 18p, 86p, Hill 34 Ref: M Scott	Gleasure Branagan	Reed Measham	Logan Kimble	Chard Smith	Wilcox Crowe	McPherson McEvoy*	Henry Butler	Benjamin Spriggs	Gilbert Cooper*	Morley Crown	Hill Kimble	Beck
								By contrast, Cambridge arrived on a roll, unbeaten in six, yet were swept away by an upbeat display which was reminiscent of early season. United were 2-0 down when Cooper was dismissed. Hill's second was his 50th for the club and took the Cobblers past 100 in league and cup.												

35	A	BURNLEY	1	L	1-2	Henry 15	Gleasure	Reed	Logan	Chard	Wilcox	McPherson	Henry	Benjamin	Gilbert	Morley	Hill
	17/3		2,682	21	82	Hoskin 39, Gallagher 70	Meenan	Leebrook	Hampton	Radaway	Gallagher	Deakin	Grewcock	Malley	Caughey	Hoskin	Britton
						Ref: K Breen	A four-man midfield had worked wonders against Cambridge, but didn't fire at Turf Moor and a lack of width was the end product. Hoskin scores against the Cobblers for the second time in the campaign. Boss Carr admits that his side got off lightly and the lead is back to 17 points.										
36	H	STOCKPORT	1	W	2-1	Chard 60, 72	Gleasure	Reed	Logan	Donald	Wilcox	McPherson	Henry*	Benjamin	Gilbert	Morley	Hill
	21/3		5,466	24	85	Entwhistle 4	Walker	Evans	Mossman	Hendrie	Matthewson	Stokes	Sartori	Moss	Entwhistle	Robinson	Chard
						Ref: J Moules	Chairman Derek Banks provided welcome fizz in the dressing room after the game. Banks was due to miss the next match with business commitments, and had decided the team were going up ... as champions. "No-one will convince me Swansea will win all their games," he said.									Brown*	Bailey
37	A	PRESTON	1	L	0-1	Brazil 10	Gleasure	Reed	Logan	Chard	Wilcox	McPherson	McGoldrick	Benjamin	Gilbert	Henry	Hill
	3/4		16,456	2	85	Ref: C Seel	Kelly	McNeil	Bennett	Atkins	Jones	Zelem	Chapman	Swann	Thomas	Brazil	Williams
							The club's first game on plastic is delayed by ten minutes to allow the crowd the chance to get in. Carlisle referee Colin Seel had also taken charge of the Newcastle FA Cup-tie, so his presence is not a positive omen. This was the only league away trip not to bring at least one goal.										
38	A	HEREFORD	1	L	2-3	Chard 26, Morley 90	Gleasure	Reed*	Logan	Donald	Wilcox	McPherson	Gilbert	Benjamin	Gilbert	Morley	Hill McGoldrick
	8/4		2,758	19	85	Phillips 25, Spoone 30, Kearns 68	Rose	Pogic	Devine	Rogers	Stevens	Dalziel*	Spooner	Carter	Phillips	Kearns	Butler Halliday
						Ref: M Reed	After an exceptional season, the Cobblers hardly deserved the Chronicle & Echo headline such as 'What A Load Of Rubbish' ... even had they lost to an amateur boys' side. In fact, skipper Morley simply shrugged his shoulders after his late consolation.										
39	H	LEYTON ORIENT	1	W	2-0	Gilbert 16, McPherson 72	Gleasure	Reed	Logan	Chard	Wilcox	McPherson	Benjamin	Benjamin	Gilbert	Morley	Hill
	12/4		6,711	10	88	Ref: J Worrall	Cass	Cunningham	Dickenson	Smalley	Howard	Cornwell	Sussex	Brooks*	Jones	Godfrey	Comfort Hales
							Cardiff's last-minute equaliser at home to Preston 24 hours earlier, and this polished Sunday best, stretched the lead to 13 points once more. Surely it was just a matter of time? Gilbert's goal meant five players (Hill, Morley, Benjamin and Chard the others) had now hit double figures.										
40	A	COLCHESTER	1	L	1-3	Logan 14	Gleasure	Reed*	Logan	Donald	Wilcox	McPherson	McGoldrick	Benjamin	Gilbert	Morley	Hill English T
	17/4		3,676	6	88	Wilkins 39, Chatterton 57p, Hedman 76	Chamberlain	English A	Norman	Chatterton	Day	Hedman	White	Adcock	Lowe	Hinshelwood	Wilkins
						Ref: C Downey	A first defeat of the season by more than one goal after an encouraging start. Logan became the 15th player to hit the target in the season. Only Gleasure of the first time squad is missing out. Carr's men had now lost four consecutive away matches in a month during a slight dip in form.										
41	H	SOUTHEND	1	W	2-1	Hill 8 McPherson 48	Gleasure	Chard	Logan	Donald	Wilcox*	McPherson	McGoldrick	Benjamin	Gilbert	Morley	Hill Reed
	20/4		7,383	3	91	Cadette 71	Stannard	Roberts	Johnson	O'Shea	Westley	Hall*	Clark	Pennyfather	Cadette	McDonough	Rogers Martin
						Ref: J McAuley	Three more points were needed for the title after The Shrimpers were left sweating on outright promotion, just a point ahead of Wolves. 'I always fancy us to beat Southend. They are an undisciplined side,' said Carr. Cadette made it five goals against Northampton in four games.										
42	A	LINCOLN	1	L	1-3	McGoldrick 65	Gleasure	Chard	Logan	Donald	Wilcox*	McPherson	McGoldrick	Benjamin	Gilbert	Morley	Hill Reed
	26/4		4,012	21	91	Gilligan 7, Gamble 51, Chard 67 (og)	Butler	Daniel	Franklin	Cooper	West	Humphries	Nicholson	Gamble*	Gilligan	Hodson	McGinlay Lund
						Ref: W Flood	A balmy Sunday at Sincil Bank turned barmy with Chard's freakish own-goal from 40 yards. This was The Imps' first home win since defeating Burnley 2-1 on 3 January, and it turned out to be their last victory before they became the inaugural victims of automatic relegation.										
43	H	CREWE	1	W	2-1	Gilbert 24p, Hill 54	Gleasure	Chard	Logan	Donald	Coy	McPherson	Benjamin	Benjamin	Gilbert	Morley	Hill
	29/4		8,890	16	94	Bodak 73	Parkin	Goodison	Pemberton	Thomas	Davis	Billinge	Platt	Bodak	Power	Wright	Cutter
						Ref: M Cotton	The title is finally sewn up to the immense relief of one and all. The Mayor of Northampton, Cllr Cyril Benton, is present to meet manager Carr and chairman Banks on a night of high emotion and, in the case of one local football reporter, a very soggy notebook. A record 20th home win.										
44	A	CARDIFF	1	D	1-1	Benjamin 8	Gleasure	Chard	Logan	Donald	Coy	McPherson	McGoldrick	Benjamin	Gilbert	Morley	Hill
	1/5		2,682	14	95	Curtis 46	Rees	Vaughan	Ford	Wimbleton	Rogers	Boyle	Platnauer	Wheeler	Mardenborough	Curtis	Gummer
						Ref: M Heath	It proved an action-packed bank holiday fixture, with Gleasure the hero of the hour after a sensational late stop from Wimbleton. At one point in the first half it seemed he had spent more time outside his penalty box than in it in a bid to avert danger. The 100-goal target remains three away.										
45	A	ALDERSHOT	1	D	3-3	Gilbert 22, Benjamin 79, Morley 85	Gleasure	Chard	Logan	Donald	Coy	McPherson	McGoldrick	Benjamin	Gilbert	Morley	Hill
	6/5		3,377	6	96	McDonald 10, King 52, Johnson 80	Coles	Mazzon	Friar	King	Smith	Wignall	Barnes	Burvill	Langley	McDonald	Ring* Johnson
						Ref: P Vanes	Ton up! Ironic that the Cobblers ended a starvation diet of goals at Aldershot. A statistic of just four goals at the Recreation Ground in ten league visits became 11 in four trips over the next four seasons! The Shots were destined for play-off glory.										
46	A	WREXHAM	1	W	3-1	Bunce 15, Morley 31, 85	Gleasure	Coy	Chard	Wilcox	McPherson	Bunce	Benjamin	Gilbert	Morley	Hill	
	9/5		2,709	9	99	Buxton 87	Salmon	Salathiel	Wright	Cunnington	Cooke	Comstive	Horne	Steele	Charles	Preece	Bunce Johnson
						Ref: P Tyldesley	The Robins' match programme Review fittingly labelled Carr's men 'Champions' on the back-page team-check as the season ended on a high note. A 30th league win of the season established a new club record, while the 47 away goals was a best ever and the total of 103 third best.										

Home 6,316 Away 4,367 Average 4,367

LEAGUE DIVISION 4 (CUP-TIES)   Manager: Graham Carr   SEASON 1986-87

Littlewoods Cup

				F-A	H-T	Scorers, Times, and Referees	1	2	3	4	5	6	7	8	9	10	11	subs used
1:1	A	GILLINGHAM	7 L 2,945 3:4	0-1	0-0	Weatherley 87 Ref: D Reeves	Gleasure Hilliard	Reed Haylock	Chard Elsey	Mann Pearce	Coy Weatherley	McPherson Oakes	McGoldrick Pritchard	Benjamin Shearer*	Gilbert Robinson	Morley Quow^	Hill Cascarino	Collins/Mayes

Donald is taken ill on the coach, so Mann steps into his shoes for this latest Cup clash with the Gills. In 1982 the Cobblers earned a home third round FA Cup-tie with Aston Villa after defeating the Kent club with a replay, although a 0-3 defeat had been the FA Cup outcome in 1985-86.

| 1:2 | H | GILLINGHAM | 4   D   2,727 3:7 | 2-2 | 1-0 | Coy 14, Benjamin 81
Cascarino 60, 84
Ref: H Taylor
(Cobblers lose 2-3 on aggregate) | Gleasure
Hillyard | Reed
Haylock | Chard
Elsey | Donald
Pearce | Coy
Weatherley | McPherson
Hinnigan | McGoldrick
Pritchard | Benjamin
Shearer | Gilbert
Robinson | Morley
Collins* | Hill
Cascarino | Quow |

The Cobblers bow out to Division Three opponents who went unbeaten in their first six league games yet were thrashed 0-6 at Division One Oxford in the first leg of the second round (drawing 1-1 at home). The Cobblers only lost 1-4 on aggregate to Oxford in the 1985-86 Milk Cup.

FA Cup

				F-A	H-T	Scorers, Times, and Referees	1	2	3	4	5	6	7	8	9	10	11	subs used
1	H	PETERBOROUGH	1 W 9,114 4:18	3-0	1-0	McGold'k 23, Gilbert 53p, Benjamin 77 Ref: T Ashworth	Gleasure Shoemake	Reed Nightingale	Gernon Collins	Mann Gunn	Wilcox Doyle	McPherson Gage	McGoldrick Paris	Benjamin Phillips	Gilbert Lawrence*	Morley Gregory	Hill Christie*	Nuttall

The rain beats down on a dismal Sunday for local rivals Posh whose goalkeeper Kevin Shoemake earns man of the match plaudits for his team, making one miraculous save from a Benjamin header. The crowd figure is boosted by a temporary stand raised on the ground's cricket side.

| 2 | A | SOUTHEND | 1   D   7,412 4:3 | 4-4 | 1-1 | Donald 7, Hill 50, 54, Benjamin 63
Cadette 8, 48, 59, McDonough 65
Ref: R Lewis | Gleasure
Stannard | Reed
Martin | Gernon
Johnson* | Donald
Roberts | Wilcox*
Westley | McPherson
Hall | McGoldrick
Clark | Benjamin
Cadette | Gilbert
McDonough | Chard
Pennyfather | Hill
Maddix | Gorman
O'Shea |

Six goals are condensed inside a frenetic 19-minute spell at the start of the second half of this Friday night epic, for which Morley is absent through injury. Wilcox goes off with a cut head early on, replaced by striker Gorman, which doesn't help the Cobblers' defensive capabilities.

| 2R | H | SOUTHEND | 1   W   10,603 3 | 3-2 | 1-2 | Benjamin 14, Gilbert 74p, 80p
Pennyfather 6, Cadette 37
Ref: R Lewis (M Penn) | Gleasure
Stannard | Reed
Martin | Chard
O'Shea | Donald
Roberts | Gernon
Westley | McPherson
Hall | McGoldrick
Clark | Benjamin
Pennyfather* | Gilbert
Cadette | Morley
McDonough | Hill
Maddix | Gymer |

The match hinges on the half-time replacement of injured referee Ray Lewis by senior linesman Penn, who awarded two home penalties. The incentive of the third-round trip to Newcastle had weighed heavily on home shoulders, with Morley's return proving crucial to the cause.

| 3 | A | NEWCASTLE | 1   L   21,177 1:22 | 1-2 | 0-1 | Hill 66
Goddard 2, Thomas A 67
Ref: C Seel | Gleasure
Thomas M | Reed
McDonald | Millar
Wharton | Donald
McCreery | Wilcox
Jackson P | McPherson
Roeder | McGoldrick
Stephenson | Benjamin
Thomas A | Chard
Goddard* | Morley*
Beardsley | Hill
Jackson D | Mann
Stewart |

Would the Cobblers have pulled off a notable FA Cup shock but for the dislocated knee injury suffered by skipper Morley? Striker Benjamin said: "I still believe we would have won but for Trevor's injury." Newcastle next beat Preston 2-0, but lost 0-1 at Tottenham in the 5th round.

158

	P	W	D	L	F	A	W	D	L	F	A	Pts
			Home						Away			
1 NORTH'TON	46	20	2	1	56	20	10	7	6	47	33	99
2 Preston	46	16	4	3	36	18	10	8	5	36	29	90
3 Southend	46	14	4	5	43	27	11	1	11	25	28	80
4 Wolves	46	12	3	8	36	24	12	4	7	33	26	79
5 Colchester	46	15	3	5	41	20	6	4	13	23	36	70
6 Aldershot *	46	13	5	5	40	22	7	5	11	24	35	70
7 Leyton Orient	46	15	2	6	40	25	5	7	11	24	36	69
8 Scunthorpe	46	15	3	5	52	27	3	9	11	21	30	66
9 Wrexham	46	8	13	2	38	24	7	7	9	32	27	65
10 Peterborough	46	10	7	6	29	21	7	7	9	28	29	65
11 Cambridge	46	12	6	5	37	23	5	5	13	25	39	62
12 Swansea	46	13	3	7	31	21	4	8	11	25	40	62
13 Cardiff	46	6	12	5	24	18	9	4	10	24	32	61
14 Exeter	46	11	10	2	37	17	0	13	10	16	32	56
15 Halifax	46	10	5	8	32	32	5	5	13	27	42	55
16 Hereford	46	10	6	7	33	23	4	5	14	27	38	53
17 Crewe	46	8	9	6	38	35	5	5	13	32	37	53
18 Hartlepool	46	6	11	6	24	30	5	5	13	20	35	51
19 Stockport	46	9	6	8	25	27	4	6	13	15	42	51
20 Tranmere	46	6	10	7	32	37	5	7	11	22	35	50
21 Rochdale	46	8	8	7	31	30	3	9	11	23	43	50
22 Burnley	46	9	7	7	31	35	3	6	14	22	39	49
23 Torquay	46	8	8	7	28	29	2	10	11	28	43	48
24 Lincoln	46	8	7	8	30	27	4	5	14	15	38	48
	1104	262	154	136	844	612	136	154	262	612	844	1502

* promoted after play-offs

Odds & ends

Double wins: (9) Torquay, Rochdale, Peterborough, Halifax, Cambridge, Stockport, Orient, Crewe, Southend.
Double losses: (1) Swansea.

Won from behind: (4) Aldershot (h), Cambridge (a), Lincoln (h), Stockp't (h).
Lost from in front: (2) Burnley (a), Colchester (a).

High spots: The 21 match unbeaten league run, stretching five months. Scoring over 100 league goals for the first time since 1962-63. Graham Carr's two Manager Of The Month awards.
Hill's 33 league and cup goal haul (one in Freight Rover Trophy). This was the best for the club since Cliff Holton's 39 in 1961-62.
Five players reaching a double-figure goal-tally.

Low spots: Losing back-to-back league games at Preston and Hereford. Third round FA Cup defeat at Newcastle, who were bottom of Division One at the time.
Morley's knee injury which kept him out for seven weeks. The side's form dipped as a consequence.

Player of the Year: Ian Benjamin.
Ever-presents: (3) Gleasure, McPherson, Benjamin.
Hat-tricks: (2) Hill.
Hat-tricks against: Halifax, Crewe.
Leading scorer: Hill (33).

	Appearances				Goals			
	Lge	Sub	LC	Sub	FAC	Sub	Lge	LC	FAC	Tot
Benjamin, Ian	46		2		4		18	1	3	22
Bunce, Paul	1	1					1			1
Chard, Phil	39		1	2	3		12			12
Coy, Bob	15	2	2						1	1
Donald, Warren	41		1		3		3		1	4
Gernon, Irvin	9				3					
Gilbert, David	45		2		3		8		3	11
Gleasure, Peter	46		2		4					
Gorman, Keith						1				
Henry, Charlie	4						1			1
Hill, Richard	45		2		4		29		3	32
Logan, David	15						1			1
Mann, Aidy	7	1	1			1				
McGoldrick, Eddie	35	4	2		4		5		1	6
McMenemy, Paul	4						2			2
McPherson, Keith	46		2		4		5			5
Millar, John	1				1					
Morley, Trevor	37		2		3		16			16
Reed, Graham	36	1	2		4		1			1
Schiavi, Mark		1				1				
Wilcox, Russell	34				3		1			1
21 players used	506	12	22		44	2	103	2	11	116

Subscribers and Their Favourite Players

John Abrams	Richard Hill
Dennis Adams	Eddie McGoldrick
Les Arnold	Trevor Morley
N Atkinson	Graham Carr
Peter Austen	
Roger Averill	Graham Carr
Julie Baker	
Richard Baker	
Bill & Betty Beesley	Trevor Morley
Graham Beesley	Richard Hill
Mary Beesley	David Gilbert
Trevor Bilson	Trevor Morley
Mark Bird	Richard Hill
Sharon (Hawkins) Boylan	Trevor Morley
David Britten	Richard Hill
The Brooker Family	Trevor Morley
Iain Brown	
Andrew Bubeer	
In memory of Peter Burdett	Keith McPherson
Richard Burke	
Les Carter	Warren Donald
Roberto Cella	
Lee Chamberlain	Richard Hill
Barrie Clarke	Richard Hill
Teresa Cogan	Graham (Rambo) Reed
Ben Coleman	Richard Hill
Keith Coleman	Trevor Morley
Paul Coles	Eddie McGoldrick
Rob Cooper	
Dave Drage	Ian Benjamin
Dick Dron	Richard Hill
Colin Eldred	Ian Benjamin
Mark Elliott	Eddie McGoldrick
Jim Finney	Trevor Morley
John Fitzhugh	Trevor Morley
Lee Fitzhugh	Peter Gleasure
Shaun Forde	
James Frampton	Ian Benjamin
Jane & Mark French	Trevor Morley
Barry & Gilly Frost	
Andrew Garden	
Chris Garden	
Lee Geary	Trevor Morley
Dave Gostelow	Ian Benjamin
Richard Gray	Ian Benjamin
Steve Hamlyn	Eddie McGoldrick
Mike Hawkes	
Les Hawkins	Trevor Morley

Subscribers and Their Favourite Players

Stephen Haynes	Richard Hill
Helen Hickman	Graham Carr
In memory of Tony Hiskey	Phil Chard
Nigel Holcombe	
Glenys & Derrick Holden	Richard Hill
Alison Holden	Ian Benjamin
Steve Hollowell	Trevor Morley
Mark Howkins	Trevor Morley
Nigel Hylands	Richard Hill
Martyn Ingram	Richard Hill
Tom Ingram	Peter Gleasure
Ian Johnson	
Kevin Johnson	
Lee Johnson	
Steve Kane	Trevor Morley
A C Kingston	Richard Hill
Barrie Kirk	Trevor Morley
Darren Lack	
Ivan Lack	
Edwin & Kieran Lane	Richard Hill
Andy Law	Ian Benjamin
Reggie Lee	
John Leeson	Richard Hill
Nigel Lemmy	Trevor Morley
Darren Lewis	
Peter Lewis	Trevor Morley
Trevor Liddle	Richard Hill
Chris Lindesay	Ian Benjamin
Nik Louch	Richard Hill
Peter Louch	Warren Donald
Gary Lovett	Ian Benjamin
John Lucas	Ian Benjamin
Ben Marlow	Trevor Morley
Calum Maclean	
Stuart McKee	Richard Hill
M J Mawby	Richard Hill
Norman & Anne Maycock	Trevor Morley
N C Miller	Trevor Morley
David Monk	Trevor Morley
Roger Monk	Graham Carr
Stan & Isa Monk	Keith McPherson
Rob Mortimer	Trevor Morley
Kevin Myers	Ian Benjamin
Tim Neath	Richard Hill
Peter Noble	Richard Hill
Simon Oliver	Richard Hill
J A Osborne	
Michael Pashler	Ian Benjamin

Subscribers and Their Favourite Players

Adam Pickup	Richard Hill
Roger Powell	Richard Hill
Andy Preekel	Trevor Morley
Clive Reece	
Karen Randall	Richard Hill
Charlotte Reed	Graham (Rambo) Reed
Olivia Reed	Graham (Rambo) Reed
Paul Richardson	
Andy Roberts	Ian Benjamin
Warren Robinson	Graham Reed
Amy Rodhouse	Richard Hill
Ben Rodhouse	Richard Hill
Steve Rodhouse	Trevor Morley
Dorothy Ronson	
Kathy Rose	Graham Carr
Sean Ruddy	Richard Hill
Martin Sargeant	Richard Hill
Graeme Andrew Scott	Richard Hill
David Sear	Trevor Morley
Richard Sear	Richard Hill
Barry Searle	Trevor Morley
Steve Simmonds	Richard Hill
David Siveter	Graham Carr
Annie Smekens	Richard Hill
C T Smith	Trevor Morley
Gerald Smith	Trevor Morley
Muray Smith	
Robert Spick	Ian Benjamin
Clive Stock	Richard Hill
Russell Sturgen	Richard Hill
Michael Sullivan	Richard Hill
Michael Tack	Richard Hill
Mike Taylor	Trevor Morley
Katie & David Toby	Trevor Morley
Mark Tucker	Richard Hill
Richard Wagg	Richard Hill
Jenny Waring	Richard Hill
Alan Watson	Richard Hill
John Watson	David Gilbert
Gary White	Richard Hill
Mick White	Trevor Morley
D Wills	Richard Hill
Graham Wills	Trevor Morley
Alan C Wright	

TWELVE DIFFERENT NAMES RECEIVED VOTES:
1ST RICHARD HILL, 2ND TREVOR MORLEY, 3RD IAN BENJAMIN